Ninja Foodi 2-Basket Air Fryer
Cookbook 2024

1500 Days Effortless, Quick & Delicious Recipes to Master the Art of Dual Zone Air Frying for Beginners Incl. 4-Week Meal Plan (Color Edition)

Ivette Jolly

Table Of
Content

Introduction

Cooking has always been my sanctuary - a place where creativity, flavors, and aromas dance together to create moments of pure joy. Over the years, my kitchen has been a laboratory of experimentation, a canvas for culinary expression. And then, the Ninja Foodi 2-Basket Air Fryer entered my culinary world, transforming it in ways I hadn't imagined.

This recipe book celebrates not just recipes, but the remarkable capabilities of this kitchen marvel. The Ninja Foodi 2-Basket Air Fryer isn't just an appliance; it's a culinary wizard that simplifies the art of cooking. Its dual baskets allow for the preparation of multiple dishes simultaneously - mains and sides harmoniously cooking together, saving time and effort in the kitchen.

Why this book? Because I believe everyone deserves the chance to create delicious, hassle-free meals. Inside these pages, you'll discover an array of recipes spanning breakfasts that kickstart your day, heartwarming meals that fill your home with comfort, delightful bread-based desserts that satisfy sweet cravings, crispy snacks that elevate snack time, and much more.

What makes this book unique? It's designed for both beginners and seasoned cooks. Detailed steps and vibrant images accompany each recipe, ensuring that regardless of your expertise, you can unleash the full potential of this incredible kitchen tool.

The Ninja Foodi 2-Basket Air Fryer isn't just about convenience; it's a gateway to culinary excellence. I invite you to join me on this gastronomic journey. Let's explore, create, and savor the magic of cooking with this remarkable appliance. With every dish you make, you'll experience the joy and ease this tool brings to the table. Let's embark on this flavorful adventure together, crafting complete and delicious meals effortlessly!

Cooking Functions

The Ninja Foodi 2-Basket Air Fryer boasts a multitude of functions, each serving as a vital tool in your culinary arsenal. These functions aren't just convenient; they're the key to unlocking a world of culinary possibilities. Let's delve into the heart of this ingenious appliance and explore the array of functions that make it an indispensable asset in the kitchen.

Now, let's take a closer look at each of these essential cooking functions:

- **Air Broil:** Providing that coveted crispy finish or gently melting toppings, the Air Broil function adds the perfect touch to your culinary creations.

- **Air Fry:** This function revolutionizes cooking by offering the crunchiness and texture you desire, all achieved with minimal to no oil, making your meals not only delicious but healthier too.

- **Roast:** Transform your Ninja Foodi into a versatile roasting oven, delivering succulent and perfectly cooked meats, vegetables, and more.

- **Reheat:** Effortlessly reheat your leftovers while maintaining their original crispy texture and flavors, ensuring that every bite feels freshly made.

- **Dehydrate:** From wholesome snacks to preserving seasonal produce, the Dehydrate function retains the goodness of meats, fruits, and vegetables, offering a healthy snacking alternative.

- **Bake:** Unleash your inner baker and create an array of delightful baked goods, from bread to desserts, with precision and ease.

These functions aren't just buttons on a panel; they're gateways to culinary mastery, designed to elevate your cooking experience. Each function serves a distinct purpose, catering to a spectrum of culinary needs and desires.

Operating Buttons

Understanding the functions and capabilities of your kitchen appliances is pivotal in mastering the art of cooking. With the Ninja Foodi 2-Basket Air Fryer, knowing the ins and outs of its operating buttons is akin to wielding a chef's most trusted tools. Let's navigate through these controls, unlocking a world of culinary potential and convenience.

Now, let's explore the essential operating buttons of the Ninja Foodi 2-Basket Air Fryer:

Basket Controls (Left): Manage the output for the left basket, offering individualized adjustments and precise control.

Basket Controls (Right): Control the output for the right basket, enabling independent settings and monitoring.

Temperature Arrows: Use these arrows to fine-tune the cooking temperature, ensuring your dishes cook at the perfect heat for optimal results.

Time Arrows: Adjust the cooking time using these arrows, providing flexibility in cooking durations across various recipes and culinary preferences.

Smart Finish Button: Automatically syncs cooking times between zones, guaranteeing both baskets finish

cooking simultaneously, regardless of differing cooking durations.

Match Cook Button: Syncs Zone 2 settings to those of Zone 1, simplifying the process for cooking larger quantities or different foods requiring the same settings.

Start/Pause Button: Initiates or pauses cooking, granting you control over the cooking process and allowing adjustments as needed.

Power Button: Serves as the master switch, turning the appliance on or off, regulating all cooking operations.

Standby Mode: After a period of inactivity, the unit enters standby mode, conserving energy with a dimly lit Power button.

Hold Mode: Ensures seamless synchronization between cooking zones while using the Smart Finish function, allowing one zone to cook while the other holds until both are ready.

Familiarizing yourself with these operating buttons is akin to wielding a chef's knife - it empowers you to craft culinary masterpieces with precision and ease. Let's delve into these controls, unveiling the key to unlocking your culinary prowess with the Ninja Foodi 2-Basket Air Fryer.

Benefits of the Ninja Foodi 2-Basket Air Fryer

1. Healthier Cooking
Air fryers use significantly less oil than traditional frying methods, reducing fat intake by up to 75% while still achieving crispy and delicious results. It's a healthier alternative for those craving fried foods.

2. Versatility
Beyond just air frying, air fryers offer multiple cooking functions like baking, roasting, air broiling, dehydrating, and reheating, making them versatile kitchen companions for a wide range of recipes.

3. Time Efficiency
With dual-zone technology, the ability to cook two different foods simultaneously or larger quantities at once saves time, streamlining meal preparation for busy households.

4. Easy Cleanup
Dishwasher-safe baskets and easily removable components make cleaning a breeze, reducing post-cooking hassle and enabling quick and convenient maintenance.

5. Temperature Control
Precise temperature settings allow for accurate cooking, ensuring that dishes are cooked evenly and to perfection every time.

6. Reduced Odors
Air fryers minimize cooking odors compared to traditional frying methods, keeping your kitchen fresher during and after cooking.

7. Energy Efficient
Air fryers generally consume less energy than conventional ovens, making them an eco-friendly choice for cooking.

8. Family-Friendly Cooking
The larger capacity of air fryers like the Ninja Foodi 2-Basket Air Fryer allows for cooking multiple servings at once, making it convenient for family meals.

9. Healthier Alternatives
Air fryers enable you to recreate your favorite fried foods with healthier ingredients, catering to dietary restrictions or preferences without compromising on taste.

10. Consistent Results
The even heat distribution and circulation in air fryers contribute to consistent cooking results, ensuring that your dishes are cooked thoroughly and uniformly.

These benefits collectively make air fryers like the Ninja Foodi 2-Basket Air Fryer not just a kitchen appliance but a valuable tool that promotes healthier, efficient, and versatile cooking experiences for home chefs.

In the realm of culinary innovation, the Ninja Foodi 2-Basket Air Fryer stands tall as a beacon of versatility, convenience, and healthier cooking. Its multifunctional capabilities, from air frying to roasting and be-

yond, offer a symphony of possibilities in the kitchen.

With the power to cook two different foods simultaneously, or handle generous portions at once, this kitchen marvel epitomizes efficiency without sacrificing taste. Its precision temperature control ensures consistent results, whether crisping up fries or baking delectable desserts.

Beyond the delectable outcomes, the Ninja Foodi 2-Basket Air Fryer embodies a commitment to healthier cooking, reducing oil usage without compromising on the coveted crispy textures we love. It's a testament to modern culinary technology that balances taste with wellness.

From simplified cleanup to reduced cooking odors, this appliance caters to the practicalities of everyday cooking, making it an indispensable ally in the kitchen. Its family-friendly capacity fosters communal dining experiences, making meal preparation an effortless joy.

Embracing the Ninja Foodi 2-Basket Air Fryer isn't just about adopting a kitchen appliance; it's about embracing a lifestyle of culinary exploration, health-conscious choices, and time-efficient meal preparation.

In essence, this remarkable tool isn't just a gadget; it's a gateway to a world of flavorful possibilities. It's an invitation to elevate your culinary prowess, streamline meal preparation, and savor the delights of healthier, tastier cooking. With the Ninja Foodi 2-Basket Air Fryer, the kitchen becomes not just a space for cooking, but a canvas for culinary artistry and effortless joy.

Chapter 1: Breakfast

Golden Avocado Tempura

SERVES 4

PREP TIME: 5 minutes
COOK TIME: 12 minutes

½ cup bread crumbs
½ tsps. salt
1 Haas avocado, pitted, peeled and sliced
Liquid from 1 can white beans

1. Mix the bread crumbs and salt in a shallow bowl until well-incorporated.
2. Dip the avocado slices in the bean liquid, then into the bread crumbs.
3. Install a crisper plate in a basket. Place avocado slices in the basket, taking care not to overlap any slices, then insert basket in unit.
4. Select Zone 1, select AIR FRY, set temperature to 350°F, and set time to 12 minutes. Press the START/PAUSE button to begin cooking.
5. With 6 minutes remaining, press START/PAUSE to pause the unit. Remove the basket from unit and shake for 10 seconds. Reinsert basket in unit and press START/PAUSE to resume cooking.
6. When cooking is complete, remove basket from unit. Transfer avocado slices to a plate. Serve warm.

Jacket Potatoes

SERVES 2

PREP TIME: 5 minutes
COOK TIME: 30 minutes

2 potatoes
1 tbsp. mozzarella cheese, shredded
1 tbsp. butter, softened
1 tsp. chives, minced
1 tbsp. fresh parsley, chopped
3 tbsps. sour cream
Salt and black pepper, to taste

1. Prick the potatoes with a fork.
2. Install a crisper plate in a basket. Place potatoes in the basket, then insert basket in unit.
3. Select Zone 1, select AIR FRY, set temperature to 400°F, and set time to 30 minutes. Press the START/PAUSE button to begin cooking.
4. With 15 minutes remaining, press START/PAUSE to pause the unit. Remove the basket from unit and flip the potatoes over. Reinsert basket in unit and press START/PAUSE to resume cooking.
5. When cooking is complete, remove basket from unit. Transfer potatoes to a plate.
6. Mix together remaining ingredients in a bowl until well combined.
7. Cut the potatoes from the center and stuff in the cheese mixture.
8. Serve immediately.

Tasty Toasts

PREP TIME: 10 minutes
COOK TIME: 6 minutes

4 bread slices
8 ounces ricotta cheese
4 ounces smoked salmon
1 shallot, sliced
1 cup arugula
1 garlic clove, minced
1 tsp. lemon zest
¼ tsp. freshly ground black pepper

1. Install a crisper plate in both baskets. Place 2 bread slices in a single layer in each basket.
2. Select Zone 1, select BAKE, set temperature to 355°F, and set time to 6 minutes. Select MATCH COOK to match Zone 2 settings to Zone 1. Select START/PAUSE to begin cooking.
3. When cooking is complete, transfer bread slices to a plate.
4. Put garlic, ricotta cheese and lemon zest in a food processor and pulse until smooth.
5. Spread this mixture over each bread slice and top with salmon, arugula and shallot.
6. Sprinkle with black pepper and serve warm.

Ham, Spinach and Egg in a Cup

SERVES 4

PREP TIME: 10 minutes
COOK TIME: 20 minutes

1 pound fresh baby spinach
4 eggs
4 tsps. milk
7-ounce ham, sliced
1 tbsp. unsalted butter, melted
1 tbsp. olive oil
Salt and black pepper, to taste

1. Grease 4 small ramekins with butter.
2. Heat olive oil in a skillet on medium heat and add baby spinach.
3. Cook for about 4 minutes and drain the liquid from the spinach completely.
4. Divide the spinach into the prepared ramekins and top with ham slices.
5. Crack 1 egg into each ramekin over ham slices and sprinkle evenly with milk. Season with salt and black pepper.
6. Install a crisper plate in both baskets. Place 2 ramekins in each basket.
7. Select Zone 1, select BAKE, set temperature to 350°F, and set time to 15 minutes. Select MATCH COOK to match Zone 2 settings to Zone 1. Select START/PAUSE to begin cooking.
8. When cooking is complete, serve warm.

Sourdough Croutons

PREP TIME: 5 minutes
COOK TIME: 6 minutes

4 cups cubed sourdough bread, 1-inch cubes
1 tbsp. olive oil
1 tsp. fresh thyme leaves
¼ tsp. salt
Freshly ground black pepper, to taste

1. Combine all ingredients in a bowl.
2. Install a crisper plate in a basket. Place bread cubes in the basket, then insert basket in unit.
3. Select Zone 1, select AIR FRY, set temperature to 400°F, and set time to 6 minutes. Press the START/PAUSE button to begin cooking.
4. With 6 minutes remaining, press START/PAUSE to pause the unit. Remove the basket from unit and shake for 10 seconds. Reinsert basket in unit and press START/PAUSE to resume cooking.
5. When cooking is complete, remove basket from unit. Transfer bread cubes to a plate. Serve warm.

Ham and Corn Muffins

PREP TIME: 10 minutes
COOK TIME: 8 minutes

¾ cup yellow cornmeal
¼ cup flour
1½ tsps. baking powder
¼ tsp. salt
1 egg, beaten
2 tbsps. canola oil
½ cup milk
½ cup shredded sharp Cheddar cheese
½ cup diced ham

1. In a medium bowl, stir together the cornmeal, flour, baking powder, and salt.
2. Add the egg, oil, and milk to dry ingredients and mix well.
3. Stir in shredded cheese and diced ham.
4. Divide batter among 8 parchment-paper-lined muffin cups.
5. Install a crisper plate in both baskets. Place 4 filled muffin cups in each basket.
6. Select Zone 1, select AIR FRY, set temperature to 390°F, and set time to 8 minutes. Select MATCH COOK to match Zone 2 settings to Zone 1. Select START/PAUSE to begin cooking, until a toothpick inserted in center of the muffin comes out clean.
7. Serve warm.

Crispy Bread Rolls

PREP TIME: 20 minutes COOK TIME: 22 minutes	5 large potatoes, boiled and mashed 2 small onions, chopped finely 2 green chilies, seeded and chopped finely 2 tbsps. fresh cilantro, chopped finely 8 bread slices, trimmed 2 tbsps. olive oil, divided ½ tsp. ground turmeric ½ tsp. mustard seeds 1 tsp. curry powder Salt, to taste

1. Heat 1 tbsp. of olive oil on medium heat in a large skillet and add mustard seeds.
2. Sauté for about 30 seconds and add onions.
3. Sauté for about 5 minutes and add curry leaves and turmeric.
4. Sauté for about 30 seconds and add the mashed potatoes and salt.
5. Mix until well combined and remove from the heat.
6. Transfer into a bowl and keep aside to cool.
7. Stir in the chilies and cilantro and divide the mixture into 8 equal-sized portions.
8. Shape each portion into an oval patty.
9. Wet the bread slices with water and squeeze the moisture with your palms.
10. Place one patty in the center of each bread slice and roll the bread around the patty.
11. Seal the edges to secure the filling and coat the rolls evenly with the remaining olive oil.
12. Install a crisper plate in both baskets. Place 4 rolls in a single layer in each basket.
13. Select Zone 1, select BAKE, set temperature to 390°F, and set time to 16 minutes. Select MATCH COOK to match Zone 2 settings to Zone 1. Select START/PAUSE to begin cooking.
14. When cooking is complete, transfer rolls to a plate. Serve warm.

Yummy Breakfast Frittata

PREP TIME: 15 minutes COOK TIME: 14 minutes	6 cherry tomatoes, halved ½ cup Parmesan cheese, grated and divided 1 bacon slice, chopped 6 fresh mushrooms, sliced 3 eggs 1 tbsp. olive oil Salt and black pepper, to taste

1. Grease a 7 x 5-inch baking dish with olive oil.
2. Mix together tomatoes, bacon, mushrooms, salt and black pepper in the baking dish.
3. Install a crisper plate in a basket. Place baking dish in the basket, then insert basket in unit.
4. Select Zone 1, select AIR FRY, set temperature to 390°F, and set time to 14 minutes. Press the START/PAUSE button to begin cooking.
5. Whisk together eggs and cheese in a bowl.
6. With 8 minutes remaining, press START/PAUSE to pause the unit. Remove the basket from unit and pour the egg mixture evenly over bacon mixture. Reinsert basket in unit and press START/PAUSE to resume cooking.
7. When cooking is complete, serve warm.

Tomato and Mozzarella Bruschetta

SERVES 2

PREP TIME: 5 minutes **COOK TIME:** 6 minutes	**6 small loaf slices** **½ cup tomatoes, finely chopped** **3 ounces (85 g) Mozzarella cheese, grated** **1 tbsp. fresh basil, chopped** **1 tbsp. olive oil**

1. Install a crisper plate in both baskets. Place 3 loaf slices in a single layer in each basket.
2. Select Zone 1, select AIR FRY, set temperature to 350°F, and set time to 6 minutes. Select MATCH COOK to match Zone 2 settings to Zone 1. Select START/PAUSE to begin cooking.
3. When the Zone 1 and 2 times reach 2 minutes, press START/PAUSE to pause the unit. Remove the baskets from unit. Add the tomato, Mozzarella, basil, and olive oil on top. Reinsert baskets in unit and press START/PAUSE to resume cooking.
4. When cooking is complete, serve warm.

Lush Vegetable Omelet

SERVES 2

PREP TIME: 10 minutes **COOK TIME:** 13 minutes	**2 tsps. canola oil** **4 eggs, whisked** **3 tbsps. plain milk** **1 tsp. melted butter** **1 red bell pepper, seeded and chopped** **1 green bell pepper, seeded and chopped** **1 white onion, finely chopped** **½ cup baby spinach leaves, roughly chopped** **½ cup Halloumi cheese, shaved** **Kosher salt and freshly ground black pepper, to taste**

1. Grease a 7 x 5-inch baking pan with canola oil.
2. Put the remaining ingredients in the baking pan and stir well.
3. Install a crisper plate in a basket. Place the baking pan in the basket, then insert basket in unit.
4. Select Zone 1, select AIR FRY, set temperature to 350°F, and set time to 13 minutes. Press the START/PAUSE button to begin cooking.
5. When cooking is complete, serve warm.

Oat and Chia Porridge

SERVES 4

PREP TIME: 10 minutes **COOK TIME:** 8 minutes	**2 tbsps. peanut butter** **4 tbsps. honey** **1 tbsp. butter, melted** **4 cups milk** **2 cups oats** **1 cup chia seeds**

1. Put the peanut butter, honey, butter, and milk in a bowl and stir to mix. Add the oats and chia seeds and stir.
2. Transfer the mixture to two 7 x 5-inch baking dish.
3. Install a crisper plate in both baskets. Place one baking dish in each basket.
4. Select Zone 1, select BAKE, set temperature to 390°F, and set time to 8 minutes. Select MATCH COOK to match Zone 2 settings to Zone 1. Select START/PAUSE to begin cooking.
5. Give another stir before serving.

Chapter 2: Fish and Seafood

Crispy Cod Cakes with Salad Greens

SERVES 4

PREP TIME: 15 minutes
COOK TIME: 13 minutes

1 pound (454 g) cod fillets, cut into chunks
⅓ cup packed fresh basil leaves
3 cloves garlic, crushed
½ tsp. smoked paprika
¼ tsp. salt
¼ tsp. pepper
1 large egg, beaten
1 cup panko bread crumbs
Cooking spray
Salad greens, for serving

1. In a food processor, pulse cod, basil, garlic, smoked paprika, salt, and pepper until cod is finely chopped, stirring occasionally. Form into 8 patties, about 2 inches in diameter. Dip each first into the egg, then into the panko, patting to adhere. Spray with oil on one side.
2. Install a crisper plate in both baskets. Place 4 cod cakes in a single layer in each basket, oil-side down; spray with oil.
3. Select Zone 1, select AIR FRY, set temperature to 390°F, and set time to 13 minutes. Select MATCH COOK to match Zone 2 settings to Zone 1. Select START/PAUSE to begin cooking.
4. When cooking is complete, transfer cod cakes to a plate. Serve with salad greens.

Cod with Asparagus

SERVES 2

PREP TIME: 15 minutes
COOK TIME: 20 minutes

2 (6-ounces) boneless cod fillets
2 tbsps. fresh parsley, roughly chopped
2 tbsps. fresh dill, roughly chopped
1 bunch asparagus
1 tsp. dried basil
1½ tbsps. fresh lemon juice
1 tbsp. olive oil
Salt and black pepper, to taste

1. Mix lemon juice, oil, basil, salt, and black pepper in a small bowl.
2. Combine the cod and ¾ of the oil mixture in another bowl.
3. Coat asparagus with remaining oil mixture.
4. Install a crisper plate in both baskets. Place cod in the Zone 1 basket, then insert basket in unit. Place asparagus in the Zone 2 basket, then insert basket in unit.
5. Select Zone 1, select AIR FRY, set temperature to 390°F, and set time to 15 minutes. Select Zone 2, select ROAST, set temperature to 390°F, and set time to 20 minutes. Select SMART FINISH. Press the START/PAUSE button to begin cooking.
6. When the Zone 1 and 2 times reach 8 minutes, press START/PAUSE to pause the unit. Remove the baskets from unit and shake for 10 seconds. Reinsert baskets in unit and press START/PAUSE to resume cooking.
7. When cooking is complete, serve cod immediately with asparagus.

Sesame Glazed Salmon

PREP TIME: 5 minutes
COOK TIME: 15 minutes

3 tbsps. soy sauce
1 tbsp. rice wine or dry sherry
1 tbsp. brown sugar
1 tbsp. toasted sesame oil
1 tsp. minced garlic
¼ tsp. minced ginger
4 (6-ounce / 170-g) salmon fillets, skin-on
½ tbsp. sesame seeds
Cooking spray

1. In a small bowl, mix the soy sauce, rice wine, brown sugar, toasted sesame oil, garlic, and ginger.
2. Place the salmon in a shallow baking dish and pour the marinade over the fillets. Cover and refrigerate for at least 1 hour, turning the fillets occasionally to coat in the marinade.
3. Install a crisper plate in both baskets. Shake off as much marinade as possible and place 2 fillets in a single layer in each basket, skin-side down. Lightly spray with cooking spray. Reserve the marinade.
4. Select Zone 1, select AIR FRY, set temperature to 390°F, and set time to 15 minutes. Select MATCH COOK to match Zone 2 settings to Zone 1. Select START/PAUSE to begin cooking.
5. When the Zone 1 and 2 times reach 8 minutes, press START/PAUSE to pause the unit. Remove the baskets from unit and flip the fillets over. Reinsert baskets in unit and press START/PAUSE to resume cooking.
6. With 3 minutes remaining, press START/PAUSE to pause the unit. Remove the baskets from unit. Brush the tops of the salmon fillets with the reserved marinade and sprinkle with sesame seeds. Reinsert baskets in unit and press START/PAUSE to resume cooking.
7. When cooking is complete, transfer salmon fillets to a plate. Serve warm.

Breaded Shrimp with Lemon

PREP TIME: 15 minutes
COOK TIME: 10 minutes

½ cup plain flour
2 egg whites
1 cup breadcrumbs
1 pound large shrimp, peeled and deveined
Salt and ground black pepper, as required
¼ tsp. lemon zest
¼ tsp. cayenne pepper
¼ tsp. red pepper flakes, crushed
2 tbsps. olive oil

1. Mix flour, salt, and black pepper in a shallow bowl.
2. Whisk the egg whites in a second bowl and mix the breadcrumbs, lime zest and spices in a third bowl.
3. Coat each shrimp with the flour, dip into egg whites and finally, dredge in the breadcrumbs. Drizzle the shrimp evenly with olive oil.
4. Install a crisper plate in both baskets. Place half of the coated shrimps in a single layer in each basket.
5. Select Zone 1, select AIR FRY, set temperature to 400°F, and set time to 10 minutes. Select MATCH COOK to match Zone 2 settings to Zone 1. Select START/PAUSE to begin cooking.
6. When the Zone 1 and 2 times reach 5 minutes, press START/PAUSE to pause the unit. Remove the baskets from unit and flip the shrimps over. Reinsert baskets in unit and press START/PAUSE to resume cooking.
7. When cooking is complete, transfer shrimps to a plate. Serve hot.

Super-Simple Scallops

SERVES 2

PREP TIME: 10 minutes
COOK TIME: 8 minutes

¾ pound sea scallops
1 tbsp. butter, melted
½ tbsp. fresh thyme, minced
Salt and black pepper, to taste

1. Mix all the ingredients in a bowl and toss to coat well.
2. Install a crisper plate in a basket. Place scallops in the basket, then insert basket in unit.
3. Select Zone 1, select AIR FRY, set temperature to 390°F, and set time to 8 minutes. Press the START/PAUSE button to begin cooking.
4. With 4 minutes remaining, press START/PAUSE to pause the unit. Remove the basket from unit and flip the fish scallops over. Reinsert basket in unit and press START/PAUSE to resume cooking.
5. When cooking is complete, remove basket from unit. Transfer scallops to a plate. Serve warm.

Simple Salmon Patty Bites

SERVES 4

PREP TIME: 15 minutes
COOK TIME: 15 minutes

4 (5-ounce / 142-g) cans pink salmon, skinless, boneless in water, drained
2 eggs, beaten
1 cup whole-wheat panko bread crumbs
4 tbsps. finely minced red bell pepper
2 tbsps. parsley flakes
2 tsps. Old Bay seasoning
Cooking spray

1. In a medium bowl, mix the salmon, eggs, panko bread crumbs, red bell pepper, parsley flakes, and Old Bay seasoning.
2. Using a small cookie scoop, form the mixture into 20 balls.
3. Install a crisper plate in both baskets. Place half of salmon bites in a single layer in each basket. Spray lightly with cooking spray.
4. Select Zone 1, select AIR FRY, set temperature to 390°F, and set time to 15 minutes. Select MATCH COOK to match Zone 2 settings to Zone 1. Select START/PAUSE to begin cooking.
5. When the Zone 1 and 2 times reach 8 minutes, press START/PAUSE to pause the unit. Remove the baskets from unit and flip the salmon bites over. Lightly spray with the cooking spray. Reinsert baskets in unit and press START/PAUSE to resume cooking.
6. When cooking is complete, transfer salmon bites to a plate. Serve warm.

Amazing Salmon Fillets

SERVES 2

PREP TIME: 5 minutes COOK TIME: 12 minutes	2 (7-ounce) (¾-inch thick) salmon fillets 1 tbsp. Italian seasoning 1 tbsp. fresh lemon juice

1. Rub the salmon evenly with Italian seasoning.
2. Install a crisper plate in a basket. Place salmon in the basket, then insert basket in unit.
3. Select Zone 1, select AIR FRY, set temperature to 400°F, and set time to 12 minutes. Press the START/PAUSE button to begin cooking.
4. When cooking is complete, remove basket from unit. Transfer salmon to a plate and squeeze lemon juice on it to serve.

Herbed Haddock

SERVES 2

PREP TIME: 10 minutes COOK TIME: 10 minutes	2 (6-ounce) haddock fillets 2 tbsps. pine nuts 3 tbsps. fresh basil, chopped 1 tbsp. Parmesan cheese, grated ½ cup extra-virgin olive oil Salt and black pepper, to taste

1. Coat the haddock fillets evenly with olive oil and season with salt and black pepper.
2. Install a crisper plate in a basket. Place haddock fillets in the basket, then insert basket in unit.
3. Select Zone 1, select ROAST, set temperature to 400°F, and set time to 10 minutes. Press the START/PAUSE button to begin cooking.
4. When cooking is complete, remove basket from unit. Transfer haddock fillets to a plate.
5. Meanwhile, put remaining ingredients in a food processor and pulse until smooth.
6. Top this cheese sauce over the haddock fillets and serve hot.

Garlic-Lemon Tilapia

SERVES 4

PREP TIME: 5 minutes COOK TIME: 15 minutes	1 tbsp. lemon juice 1 tbsp. olive oil 1 tsp. minced garlic ½ tsp. chili powder 4 (6-ounce / 170-g) tilapia fillets

1. In a large, shallow bowl, mix together the lemon juice, olive oil, garlic, and chili powder to make a marinade. Place the tilapia fillets in the bowl and coat evenly.
2. Install a crisper plate in both baskets. Place 2 tilapia fillets in a single layer in each basket, leaving space between each fillet.
3. Select Zone 1, select AIR FRY, set temperature to 400°F, and set time to 15 minutes. Select MATCH COOK to match Zone 2 settings to Zone 1. Select START/PAUSE to begin cooking, until the fish is cooked and flakes easily with a fork.
4. When cooking is complete, transfer tilapia fillets to a plate. Serve warm.

Cod and Veggies

PREP TIME: 20 minutes
COOK TIME: 25 minutes

2 tbsps. butter, melted
½ cup red bell peppers, seeded and thinly sliced
½ cup carrots, peeled and julienned
½ cup fennel bulbs, julienned
2 (5-ounces) frozen cod fillets, thawed
1 tbsp. fresh lemon juice
½ tsp. dried tarragon
Salt and ground black pepper, as required
1 tbsp. olive oil

1. Mix butter, lemon juice, tarragon, salt, and black pepper in a large bowl.
2. Add the carrot, bell pepper and fennel bulb and generously coat with the butter mixture.
3. Coat the cod fillets with olive oil and season with salt and black pepper. Top with any remaining sauce from the bowl.
4. Install a crisper plate in both baskets. Place cod fillets in the Zone 1 basket, then insert basket in unit. Place vegetables in the Zone 2 basket, then insert basket in unit.
5. Select Zone 1, select AIR FRY, set temperature to 390°F, and set time to 15 minutes. Select Zone 2, select AIR FRY, set temperature to 390°F, and set time to 25 minutes. Select SMART FINISH. Press the START/PAUSE button to begin cooking.
6. When zones have finished cooking, check cod fillets for doneness. Transfer cod fillets to a plate and serve with vegetables.

Cod Cakes

PREP TIME: 20 minutes
COOK TIME: 10 minutes

1 pound cod fillet
1 egg
⅓ cup coconut, grated and divided
1 scallion, finely chopped
2 tbsps. fresh parsley, chopped
1 tsp. fresh lime zest, finely grated
1 tsp. red chili paste
Salt, as required
1 tbsp. fresh lime juice

1. Put the cod fillet, lime zest, egg, chili paste, salt and lime juice in a food processor and pulse until smooth.
2. Transfer the cod mixture into a bowl and add scallion, parsley and 2 tbsps. of coconut.
3. Mix until well combined and make 12 equal-sized round cakes from the mixture.
4. Place the remaining coconut in a shallow bowl and coat the cod cakes with coconut.
5. Install a crisper plate in both baskets. Place half of cod cakes in a single layer in each basket.
6. Select Zone 1, select AIR FRY, set temperature to 390°F, and set time to 10 minutes. Select MATCH COOK to match Zone 2 settings to Zone 1. Select START/PAUSE to begin cooking.
7. When the Zone 1 and 2 times reach 5 minutes, press START/PAUSE to pause the unit. Remove the baskets from unit and flip the cod cakes over. Reinsert baskets in unit and press START/PAUSE to resume cooking.
8. When cooking is complete, transfer cod cakes to a plate. Serve warm.

Chapter 3: Poultry

Chicken with Broccoli

PREP TIME: 20 minutes
COOK TIME: 18 minutes

1 pound boneless, skinless chicken breasts, sliced
1½ cups small broccoli florets
1/6 cup butter
1½ tbsps. dried parsley, crushed
½ tbsp. onion powder
½ tbsp. garlic powder
¼ tsp. red chili powder
¼ tsp. paprika

1. Mix the butter, parsley and spices in a bowl.
2. Coat the chicken slices and broccoli generously with the spice mixture.
3. Install a crisper plate in both baskets. Place marinated chicken slices in the Zone 1 basket, then insert basket in unit. Place broccoli in the Zone 2 basket, then insert basket in unit.
4. Select Zone 1, select AIR FRY, set temperature to 390°F, and set time to 18 minutes. Select Zone 2, select AIR FRY, set temperature to 390°F, and set time to 15 minutes. Select SMART FINISH. Press the START/PAUSE button to begin cooking.
5. When the Zone 1 and 2 times reach 8 minutes, press START/PAUSE to pause the unit. Remove the baskets from unit and shake for 10 seconds. Reinsert baskets in unit and press START/PAUSE to resume cooking.
6. When cooking is complete, serve chicken with broccoli.

Herbed Turkey Breast

PREP TIME: 15 minutes
COOK TIME: 40 minutes

1 (2½-pounds) bone-in, skin-on turkey breast
1 tsp. dried thyme, crushed
1 tsp. dried rosemary, crushed
½ tsp. dried sage, crushed
½ tsp. dark brown sugar
½ tsp. garlic powder
½ tsp. paprika
1 tbsp. olive oil

1. Mix the herbs, brown sugar, and spices in a bowl.
2. Drizzle the turkey breast with oil and season with the herb mixture.
3. Install a crisper plate in a basket. Place turkey breast in the basket, then insert basket in unit.
4. Select Zone 1, select ROAST, set temperature to 390°F, and set time to 40 minutes. Press the START/PAUSE button to begin cooking.
5. With 20 minutes remaining, press START/PAUSE to pause the unit. Remove the basket from unit and flip the turkey breast over. Reinsert basket in unit and press START/PAUSE to resume cooking.
6. When cooking is complete, remove basket from unit. Transfer turkey breast to a plate and cut into desired size slices to serve.

Air Fried Crispy Chicken Tenders

SERVES 3

PREP TIME: 20 minutes
COOK TIME: 24 minutes

2 (6-ounces) boneless, skinless chicken breasts, pounded into ½-inch thickness and cut into tenders
½ cup all-purpose flour
1½ cups panko breadcrumbs
¼ cup Parmesan cheese, finely grated
2 large eggs
1½ tsps. Worcestershire sauce, divided
¾ cup buttermilk
½ tsp. smoked paprika, divided
Salt and ground black pepper, as required

1. Mix buttermilk, ¾ tsp. of Worcestershire sauce, ¼ tsp. of paprika, salt, and black pepper in a bowl.
2. Combine the flour, remaining paprika, salt, and black pepper in another bowl.
3. Whisk the egg and remaining Worcestershire sauce in a third bowl.
4. Mix the panko breadcrumbs and Parmesan cheese in a fourth bowl.
5. Put the chicken tenders into the buttermilk mixture and refrigerate overnight.
6. Remove the chicken tenders from the buttermilk mixture and dredge into the flour mixture.
7. Dip into the egg and coat with the breadcrumb mixture.
8. Install a crisper plate in both baskets. Place half of the chicken tenders in a single layer in each basket.
9. Select Zone 1, select AIR FRY, set temperature to 390°F, and set time to 24 minutes. Select MATCH COOK to match Zone 2 settings to Zone 1. Select START/PAUSE to begin cooking.
10. When the Zone 1 and 2 times reach 12 minutes, press START/PAUSE to pause the unit. Remove the baskets from unit and flip the chicken tenders over. Reinsert baskets in unit and press START/PAUSE to resume cooking.
11. When cooking is complete, transfer chicken tenders to a plate. Serve warm.

Spinach Stuffed Chicken Breasts

SERVES 2

PREP TIME: 15 minutes
COOK TIME: 29 minutes

1¾ ounces fresh spinach
¼ cup ricotta cheese, shredded
2 (4-ounces) skinless, boneless chicken breasts
2 tbsps. cheddar cheese, grated
1 tbsp. olive oil
Salt and ground black pepper, as required
¼ tsp. paprika

1. Heat olive oil in a medium skillet over medium heat and cook spinach for about 4 minutes.
2. Add the ricotta and cook for about 1 minute.
3. Cut the slits in each chicken breast horizontally and stuff with the spinach mixture.
4. Season each chicken breast evenly with salt and black pepper and top with cheddar cheese and paprika.
5. Install a crisper plate in a basket. Place chicken breasts in the basket, then insert basket in unit.
6. Select Zone 1, select AIR FRY, set temperature to 390°F, and set time to 25 minutes. Press the START/PAUSE button to begin cooking.
7. When cooking is complete, remove basket from unit. Transfer chicken breasts to a plate. Serve warm.

Buffalo Chicken Tenders

SERVES 3

PREP TIME: 20 minutes
COOK TIME: 24 minutes

1 tbsp. water
1 large egg
16 ounces boneless, skinless chicken breasts, sliced into tenders
½ cup pork rinds, crushed
2 tbsps. butter, melted
½ cup unflavored whey protein powder
½ tsp. garlic powder
Salt and ground black pepper, as required
¼ cup buffalo wing sauce

1. Whisk the egg and water in a bowl and coat the chicken with it.
2. Mix the pork rinds, protein powder, garlic powder, salt, and black pepper in another bowl.
3. Coat the chicken tenders with the pork rinds mixture. Install a crisper plate in both baskets. Place half of chicken tenders in a single layer in each basket. Drizzle with the melted butter.
4. Select Zone 1, select AIR FRY, set temperature to 390°F, and set time to 24 minutes. Select MATCH COOK to match Zone 2 settings to Zone 1. Select START/PAUSE to begin cooking.
5. When the Zone 1 and 2 times reach 10 minutes, press START/PAUSE to pause the unit. Remove the baskets from unit and flip the chicken tenders over. Reinsert baskets in unit and press START/PAUSE to resume cooking.
6. When cooking is complete, transfer chicken tenders to a plate. Top with the buffalo sauce to serve hot.

Spicy Chicken Legs

SERVES 3

PREP TIME: 15 minutes
COOK TIME: 22 minutes

3 (8-ounces) chicken legs
1 cup buttermilk
2 cups white flour
1 tsp. garlic powder
1 tsp. onion powder
1 tsp. ground cumin
1 tsp. paprika
Salt and ground black pepper, as required
1 tbsp. olive oil

1. Mix the chicken legs, and buttermilk in a bowl and refrigerate for about 2 hours.
2. Combine the flour and spices in another bowl and dredge the chicken legs into this mixture.
3. Now, dip the chicken into the buttermilk and coat again with the flour mixture.
4. Install a crisper plate in a basket. Place chicken legs in the basket and drizzle with the oil, then insert basket in unit.
5. Select Zone 1, select ROAST, set temperature to 390°F, and set time to 22 minutes. Press the START/PAUSE button to begin cooking.
6. With 10 minutes remaining, press START/PAUSE to pause the unit. Remove the basket from unit and flip the chicken legs over. Reinsert basket in unit and press START/PAUSE to resume cooking.
7. When cooking is complete, remove basket from unit. Transfer chicken legs to a plate. Serve warm.

Sweet and Sour Chicken Thighs

SERVES 2

PREP TIME: 15 minutes COOK TIME: 20 minutes	1 scallion, finely chopped 2 (4-ounces) skinless, boneless chicken thighs ½ cup corn flour 1 garlic clove, minced	½ tbsp. soy sauce ½ tbsp. rice vinegar 1 tsp. sugar Salt and black pepper, as required

1. Mix all the ingredients except chicken and corn flour in a bowl.
2. Place the corn flour in another bowl.
3. Coat the chicken thighs into the marinade and then dredge into the corn flour.
4. Install a crisper plate in a basket. Place chicken thighs in the basket, skin side down, then insert basket in unit.
5. Select Zone 1, select AIR FRY, set temperature to 390°F, and set time to 20 minutes. Press the START/PAUSE button to begin cooking.
6. With 10 minutes remaining, press START/PAUSE to pause the unit. Remove the basket from unit and flip the chicken thighs over. Reinsert basket in unit and press START/PAUSE to resume cooking.
7. When cooking is complete, remove basket from unit. Transfer chicken thighs to a plate. Serve warm.

Oats Crusted Chicken Breasts

SERVES 2

PREP TIME: 20 minutes COOK TIME: 22 minutes	2 (6-ounces) chicken breasts ¾ cup oats 1 tbsp. fresh parsley	2 medium eggs Salt and black pepper, to taste 2 tbsps. mustard powder

1. Season the chicken pieces with salt and black pepper and keep aside.
2. Put the oats, mustard powder, parsley, salt and black pepper in a blender and pulse until coarse.
3. Place the oat mixture into a shallow bowl and whisk the eggs in another bowl.
4. Dredge the chicken in the oat mixture and dip into the whisked eggs.
5. Install a crisper plate in a basket. Place chicken breasts in the basket, then insert basket in unit.
6. Select Zone 1, select AIR FRY, set temperature to 390°F, and set time to 22 minutes. Press the START/PAUSE button to begin cooking.
7. With 10 minutes remaining, press START/PAUSE to pause the unit. Remove the basket from unit and flip the chicken breasts over. Reinsert basket in unit and press START/PAUSE to resume cooking.
8. When cooking is complete, remove basket from unit. Transfer chicken breasts to a plate. Serve warm.

Simple Chicken Wings and Cauliflower

SERVES 2

PREP TIME: 10 minutes COOK TIME: 30 minutes	1 pound chicken wings Salt and black pepper, to taste 1½ cups cauliflower, cut into 1-inch pieces 1 tbsp. olive oil

1. Season the chicken wings evenly with salt and black pepper.
2. Mix the vegetables, olive oil, and salt in a bowl and toss to coat well.
3. Install a crisper plate in both baskets. Place chicken wings in the Zone 1 basket, then insert basket in unit. Place vegetables in the Zone 2 basket, then insert basket in unit.
4. Select Zone 1, select AIR FRY, set temperature to 390°F, and set time to 30 minutes. Select Zone 2, select ROAST, set temperature to 390°F, and set time to 20 minutes. Select SMART FINISH. Press the START/PAUSE button to begin cooking.
5. When the Zone 1 and Zone 2 times reach 10 minutes, press START/PAUSE and remove baskets from unit. In Zone 1, flip the chicken wings over. In Zone 2, shake for 10 seconds. Reinsert baskets in unit and press START/PAUSE to resume cooking.
6. When cooking is complete, serve chicken wings with vegetables.

Crispy Chicken Drumsticks

PREP TIME: 15 minutes COOK TIME: 22 minutes	4 (4-ounces) chicken drumsticks ½ cup buttermilk ½ cup all-purpose flour ½ cup panko breadcrumbs 3 tbsps. butter, melted ¼ tsp. baking powder ¼ tsp. dried oregano	¼ tsp. dried thyme ¼ tsp. celery salt ¼ tsp. garlic powder ¼ tsp. ground ginger ¼ tsp. cayenne pepper ¼ tsp. paprika Salt and ground black pepper, as required

1. Put the chicken drumsticks and buttermilk in a resealable plastic bag.
2. Seal the bag tightly and refrigerate for about 3 hours.
3. Mix the flour, breadcrumbs, baking powder, herbs and spices in a bowl.
4. Remove the chicken drumsticks from bag and coat chicken drumsticks evenly with the seasoned flour mixture.
5. Install a crisper plate in a basket. Place chicken drumsticks in the basket, then insert basket in unit.
6. Select Zone 1, select AIR FRY, set temperature to 390°F, and set time to 22 minutes. Press the START/PAUSE button to begin cooking.
7. With 10 minutes remaining, press START/PAUSE to pause the unit. Remove the basket from unit and flip the chicken drumsticks over. Reinsert basket in unit and press START/PAUSE to resume cooking.
8. When cooking is complete, remove basket from unit. Transfer chicken drumsticks to a plate. Serve warm.

Parmesan Chicken Cutlets with Mushroom

PREP TIME: 15 minutes COOK TIME: 30 minutes	¾ cup all-purpose flour 2 large eggs 1½ cups panko breadcrumbs ¼ cup Parmesan cheese, grated 4 (6-ounces) (¼-inch thick) skinless, boneless chicken cutlets 1 tbsp. mustard powder Salt and black pepper, to taste 8 ounces cremini mushrooms, halved 2 tbsps. soy sauce 2 tbsps. maple syrup 2 tbsps. rice vinegar 2 garlic cloves, finely chopped

1. Place the flour in a shallow bowl and whisk the eggs in a second bowl.
2. Mix the breadcrumbs, cheese, mustard powder, salt, and black pepper in a third bowl.
3. Season the chicken with salt and black pepper and coat the chicken with flour.
4. Dip the chicken into whisked eggs and finally dredge into the breadcrumb mixture.
5. Install a crisper plate in both baskets. Place the chicken cutlets in the Zone 1 basket, then insert basket in unit. Place mushrooms in the Zone 2 basket, then insert basket in unit.
6. Select Zone 1, select AIR FRY, set temperature to 390°F, and set time to 30 minutes. Select Zone 2, select ROAST, set temperature to 390°F, and set time to 15 minutes. Select SMART FINISH. Press the START/PAUSE button to begin cooking.
7. Meanwhile, mix soy sauce, maple syrup, vinegar and garlic in a bowl.
8. When the Zone 1 and Zone 2 times reach 8 minutes, press START/PAUSE and remove baskets from unit. In Zone 1, flip the chicken over. In Zone 2, Spread the soy sauce mixture over the mushrooms. Reinsert baskets in unit and press START/PAUSE to resume cooking.
9. When cooking is complete, serve chicken with mushrooms.

Chapter 4: Vegetables

Sweet and Sour Brussels Sprouts

SERVES 2

PREP TIME: 10 minutes
COOK TIME: 16 minutes

2 cups Brussels sprouts, trimmed and halved lengthwise
1 tbsp. balsamic vinegar
1 tbsp. maple syrup
Salt, as required

1. Mix all the ingredients in a bowl and toss to coat well.
2. Install a crisper plate in a basket. Place Brussels sprouts in the basket, then insert basket in unit.
3. Select Zone 1, select AIR FRY, set temperature to 400°F, and set time to 16 minutes. Press the START/PAUSE button to begin cooking.
4. With 8 minutes remaining, press START/PAUSE to pause the unit. Remove the basket from unit and flip the Brussels sprouts over. Reinsert basket in unit and press START/PAUSE to resume cooking.
5. When cooking is complete, remove basket from unit. Transfer Brussels sprouts to a plate. Serve warm.

Parmesan Asparagus

SERVES 3

PREP TIME: 15 minutes
COOK TIME: 22 minutes

1 pound fresh asparagus, trimmed
1 tbsp. Parmesan cheese, grated
1 tbsp. butter, melted
1 tsp. garlic powder
Salt and black pepper, to taste

1. Mix the asparagus, cheese, butter, garlic powder, salt, and black pepper in a bowl and toss to coat well.
2. Install a crisper plate in a basket. Place asparagus in the basket, then insert basket in unit.
3. Select Zone 1, select ROAST, set temperature to 390°F, and set time to 22 minutes. Press the START/PAUSE button to begin cooking.
4. With 10 minutes remaining, press START/PAUSE to pause the unit. Remove the basket from unit and shake for 10 seconds. Reinsert basket in unit and press START/PAUSE to resume cooking.
5. When cooking is complete, remove basket from unit. Transfer asparagus to a plate. Serve warm.

Crispy Bacon-Wrapped Asparagus Bundles

SERVES 4

PREP TIME: 20 minutes
COOK TIME: 10 minutes

1 pound asparagus
4 bacon slices
½ tbsp. sesame seeds, toasted
1 garlic clove, minced
1½ tbsps. brown sugar
1½ tbsps. olive oil
½ tbsp. sesame oil, toasted

1. Mix garlic, brown sugar, olive oil and sesame oil in a bowl till sugar is dissolved.
2. Divide asparagus into 4 equal bunches and wrap a bacon slice around each bunch.
3. Rub the asparagus bunch with garlic mixture.
4. Install a crisper plate in a basket. Place asparagus bunches in the basket and sprinkle with sesame seeds, then insert basket in unit.
5. Select Zone 1, select ROAST, set temperature to 390°F, and set time to 10 minutes. Press the START/PAUSE button to begin cooking.
6. With 5 minutes remaining, press START/PAUSE to pause the unit. Remove the basket from unit and flip the asparagus bunches over. Reinsert basket in unit and press START/PAUSE to resume cooking.
7. When cooking is complete, remove basket from unit. Transfer asparagus bunches to a plate. Serve warm.

Caramelized Carrots

SERVES 3

PREP TIME: 10 minutes
COOK TIME: 15 minutes

1 small bag baby carrots
½ cup butter, melted
½ cup brown sugar

1. Mix the butter and brown sugar in a bowl.
2. Add the carrots and toss to coat well.
3. Install a crisper plate in a basket. Place carrots in the basket, then insert basket in unit.
4. Select Zone 1, select AIR FRY, set temperature to 390°F, and set time to 15 minutes. Press the START/PAUSE button to begin cooking.
5. With 8 minutes remaining, press START/PAUSE to pause the unit. Remove the basket from unit and flip the carrots over. Reinsert basket in unit and press START/PAUSE to resume cooking.
6. When cooking is complete, remove basket from unit. Transfer carrots to a plate. Serve warm.

Spices Stuffed Eggplants

PREP TIME: 15 minutes
COOK TIME: 15 minutes

8 baby eggplants
4 tsps. olive oil, divided
¾ tbsp. dry mango powder
¾ tbsp. ground coriander
½ tsp. ground cumin
½ tsp. ground turmeric
½ tsp. garlic powder
Salt, to taste

1. Make 2 slits from the bottom of each eggplant leaving the stems intact.
2. Add 1 tsp. of oil, mango powder, coriander, cumin, turmeric and garlic powder in a bowl, mix well.
3. Fill each slit of eggplants with this spices mixture. Brush the outer side of each eggplant with remaining oil.
4. Install a crisper plate in both baskets. Place half of the eggplants in a single layer in each basket.
5. Select Zone 1, select AIR FRY, set temperature to 370°F, and set time to 15 minutes. Select MATCH COOK to match Zone 2 settings to Zone 1. Select START/PAUSE to begin cooking.
6. When cooking is complete, transfer eggplants to a plate. Serve warm.

Broccoli with Olives

PREP TIME: 15 minutes
COOK TIME: 19 minutes

2 pounds broccoli, stemmed and cut into 1-inch florets
⅓ cup Kalamata olives, halved and pitted
¼ cup Parmesan cheese, grated
2 tbsps. olive oil
Salt and ground black pepper, as required
2 tsps. fresh lemon zest, grated

1. Boil the broccoli in a pot for about 4 minutes and drain well.
2. Mix broccoli, oil, salt, and black pepper in a bowl and toss to coat well.
3. Install a crisper plate in a basket. Place broccoli in the basket, then insert basket in unit.
4. Select Zone 1, select AIR FRY, set temperature to 390°F, and set time to 15 minutes. Press the START/PAUSE button to begin cooking.
5. With 8 minutes remaining, press START/PAUSE to pause the unit. Remove the basket from unit and shake for 10 seconds. Reinsert basket in unit and press START/PAUSE to resume cooking.
6. When cooking is complete, remove basket from unit. Transfer broccoli to a plate. Stir in the olives, lemon zest and cheese and dish out to serve.

Garden Fresh Veggie Medley

SERVES 4

PREP TIME: 10 minutes COOK TIME: 25 minutes	2 yellow bell peppers, seeded and chopped 1 eggplant, chopped 1 zucchini, chopped 3 tomatoes, chopped 2 small onions, chopped 2 garlic cloves, minced 2 tbsps. herbs de Provence 1 tbsp. olive oil 1 tbsp. balsamic vinegar Salt and black pepper, to taste

1. Mix all the ingredients in a bowl and toss to coat well.
2. Install a crisper plate in both baskets. Place half of the vegetables in a single layer in each basket.
3. Select Zone 1, select AIR FRY, set temperature to 390°F, and set time to 25 minutes. Select MATCH COOK to match Zone 2 settings to Zone 1. Select START/PAUSE to begin cooking.
4. When the Zone 1 and 2 times reach 12 minutes, press START/PAUSE to pause the unit. Remove the baskets from unit and flip vegetables over. Reinsert baskets in unit and press START/PAUSE to resume cooking.
5. When cooking is complete, transfer vegetables to a plate. Serve warm.

Potato Salad

SERVES 6

PREP TIME: 10 minutes COOK TIME: 40 minutes	4 Russet potatoes 3 hard-boiled eggs, peeled and chopped 1 cup celery, chopped ½ cup red onion, chopped 1 tbsp. olive oil Salt, as required 1 tbsp. prepared mustard ¼ tsp. celery salt ¼ tsp. garlic salt ¼ cup mayonnaise

1. Prick the potatoes with a fork and rub with olive oil and salt.
2. Install a crisper plate in a basket. Place potatoes in the basket, then insert basket in unit.
3. Select Zone 1, select ROAST, set temperature to 400°F, and set time to 40 minutes. Press the START/PAUSE button to begin cooking.
4. When cooking is complete, remove basket from unit. Transfer potatoes to a plate and keep aside to cool.
5. Add the remaining ingredients and mix well.
6. Refrigerate for about 2 hours and serve immediately.

Perfectly Roasted Mushrooms

SERVES 4

PREP TIME: 10 minutes COOK TIME: 25 minutes	1 tbsp. butter, melted 2 pounds mushrooms, quartered 2 tbsps. white vermouth 2 tsps. herbs de Provence ½ tsp. garlic powder

1. Mix herbs de Provence, garlic powder and butter and mushrooms in a large bowl.
2. Install a crisper plate in both baskets. Place half of the mushrooms in a single layer in each basket.
3. Select Zone 1, select AIR FRY, set temperature to 390°F, and set time to 25 minutes. Select MATCH COOK to match Zone 2 settings to Zone 1. Select START/PAUSE to begin cooking.
4. When the Zone 1 and 2 times reach 5 minutes, press START/PAUSE to pause the unit. Remove the baskets from unit and stir the mushrooms with white vermouth. Reinsert baskets in unit and press START/PAUSE to resume cooking.
5. When cooking is complete, transfer the mushrooms to a plate. Serve warm.

Okra with Green Beans

SERVES 2

PREP TIME: 10 minutes COOK TIME: 20 minutes	½ (10-ounces) bag frozen cut okra ½ (10-ounces) bag frozen cut green beans ¼ cup nutritional yeast 3 tbsps. balsamic vinegar Salt and black pepper, to taste

1. Mix the okra, green beans, nutritional yeast, vinegar, salt, and black pepper in a bowl and toss to coat well.
2. Install a crisper plate in both baskets. Place half of the okra mixture in each basket.
3. Select Zone 1, select AIR FRY, set temperature to 390°F, and set time to 20 minutes. Select MATCH COOK to match Zone 2 settings to Zone 1. Select START/PAUSE to begin cooking.
4. When the Zone 1 and 2 times reach 10 minutes, press START/PAUSE to pause the unit. Remove the baskets from unit and shake for 10 seconds. Reinsert baskets in unit and press START/PAUSE to resume cooking.
5. When cooking is complete, transfer the okra mixture to a plate. Serve warm.

Cheesy Brussels Sprouts

SERVES 3

PREP TIME: 15 minutes COOK TIME: 15 minutes	1 pound Brussels sprouts, trimmed and halved ¼ cup whole wheat breadcrumbs ¼ cup Parmesan cheese, shredded 1 tbsp. balsamic vinegar 1 tbsp. extra-virgin olive oil Salt and black pepper, to taste

1. Mix Brussels sprouts, vinegar, oil, salt, and black pepper in a bowl and toss to coat well.
2. Install a crisper plate in a basket. Place Brussels sprouts in the basket, then insert basket in unit.
3. Select Zone 1, select AIR FRY, set temperature to 400°F, and set time to 15 minutes. Press the START/PAUSE button to begin cooking.
4. With 5 minutes remaining, press START/PAUSE to pause the unit. Remove the basket from unit. Sprinkle with breadcrumbs and cheese. Reinsert basket in unit and press START/PAUSE to resume cooking.
5. When cooking is complete, remove basket from unit. Transfer Brussels sprouts to a plate. Serve warm.

Chapter 5: Burger and Kebabs

Beef Chuck Cheeseburgers

SERVES 4

PREP TIME: 10 minutes
COOK TIME: 12 minutes

¾ pound (340 g) ground beef chuck
1 envelope onion soup mix
Kosher salt and freshly ground black pepper, to taste
1 tsp. paprika
4 slices Monterey Jack cheese
4 ciabatta rolls

1. In a bowl, stir together the ground chuck, onion soup mix, salt, black pepper, and paprika to combine well.
2. Take four equal portions of the mixture and mold each one into a patty.
3. Install a crisper plate in both baskets. Place 2 patties in a single layer in each basket.
4. Select Zone 1, select AIR FRY, set temperature to 390°F, and set time to 12 minutes. Select MATCH COOK to match Zone 2 settings to Zone 1. Select START/PAUSE to begin cooking.
5. When the Zone 1 and 2 times reach 1 minute, press START/PAUSE to pause the unit. Remove the baskets from unit and put the slices of cheese on the top of the patties. Reinsert baskets in unit and press START/PAUSE to resume cooking.
6. When cooking is complete, transfer patties to a plate. Serve warm on ciabatta rolls.

Lamb Burger

SERVES 4

PREP TIME: 15 minutes
COOK TIME: 22-23 minutes

2 tsps. olive oil
⅓ onion, finely chopped
1 clove garlic, minced
1 pound (454 g) ground lamb
2 tbsps. fresh parsley, finely chopped
1½ tsps. fresh oregano, finely chopped
½ cup black olives, finely chopped
⅓ cup crumbled feta cheese
½ tsp. salt
freshly ground black pepper
4 thick pita breads
toppings and condiments

1. Preheat a medium skillet over medium-high heat on the stovetop. Add the olive oil and cook the onion until tender, but not browned about 4 to 5 minutes. Add the garlic and cook for another minute. Transfer the onion and garlic to a mixing bowl and add the ground lamb, parsley, oregano, olives, feta cheese, salt and pepper. Gently mix the ingredients together.
2. Divide the mixture into 4 equal portions and then form the hamburgers, being careful not to over-handle the meat. One good way to do this is to throw the meat back and forth between the hands like a baseball, packing the meat each time you catch it. Flatten the balls into patties, making an indentation in the center of each patty. Flatten the sides of the patties as well to make it easier to fit them into the air fryer basket.
3. Install a crisper plate in both baskets. Place 2 burgers in a single layer in each basket.
4. Select Zone 1, select AIR FRY, set temperature to 370°F, and set time to 16 minutes. Select MATCH COOK to match Zone 2 settings to Zone 1. Select START/PAUSE to begin cooking.
5. When the Zone 1 and 2 times reach 8 minutes, press START/PAUSE to pause the unit. Remove the baskets from unit and flip the burgers over. Reinsert baskets in unit and press START/PAUSE to resume cooking.
6. When cooking is complete, transfer burgers to a plate and let the burgers rest for a few minutes before dressing and serving.
7. While the burgers are resting, bake the pita breads in the air fryer for 2 minutes. Tuck the burgers into the toasted pita breads, or wrap the pitas around the burgers and serve with a tzatziki sauce or some mayonnaise.

Beef Cheeseburgers

SERVES 2

PREP TIME: 15 minutes
COOK TIME: 13 minutes

½ pound ground beef
2 tbsps. fresh cilantro, minced
2 slices cheddar cheese
2 salad leaves
2 dinner rolls, cut into half
1 garlic clove, minced
Salt and black pepper, to taste

1. Mix the beef, garlic, cilantro, salt, and black pepper in a bowl.
2. Make 2 equal-sized patties from the beef mixture.
3. Install a crisper plate in a basket. Place patties in the basket, then insert basket in unit.
4. Select Zone 1, select BAKE, set temperature to 390°F, and set time to 13 minutes. Press the START/PAUSE button to begin cooking.
5. When 1 minute remains, press START/PAUSE to pause the unit. Remove the basket from unit and top each patty with 1 cheese slice. Reinsert basket in unit and press START/PAUSE to resume cooking.
6. When cooking is complete, remove basket from unit. Transfer patties to a plate. Place dinner rolls in a serving platter and arrange salad leaf between each dinner roll. Top with 1 patty and immediately serve.

Sweet and Salty Chicken Kebobs

SERVES 4

PREP TIME: 20 minutes
COOK TIME: 15 minutes

4 (4-ounce) skinless, boneless chicken thighs, cubed into 1-inch size
5 scallions, cut into 1-inch pieces lengthwise
Wooden skewers, presoaked
¼ cup light soy sauce
1 tbsp. mirin
1 tsp. garlic salt
1 tsp. sugar

1. Mix soy sauce, mirin, garlic salt and sugar in a large baking dish.
2. Thread scallions and chicken onto pre-soaked wooden skewers.
3. Coat the skewers generously with marinade. Install a crisper plate in a basket. Place skewers in the basket, then insert basket in unit.
4. Select Zone 1, select ROAST, set temperature to 390°F, and set time to 15 minutes. Press the START/PAUSE button to begin cooking.
5. With 6 minutes remaining, press START/PAUSE to pause the unit. Remove the basket from unit and flip the skewers over. Reinsert basket in unit and press START/PAUSE to resume cooking.
6. When cooking is complete, remove basket from unit. Transfer skewers to a plate. Serve warm.

Spicy Lamb Kebabs

PREP TIME: 20 minutes
COOK TIME: 8 minutes

4 eggs, beaten
1 cup pistachios, chopped
1 pound ground lamb
4 tbsps. plain flour
4 tbsps. flat-leaf parsley, chopped
2 tsps. chili flakes
4 garlic cloves, minced

2 tbsps. fresh lemon juice
2 tsps. cumin seeds
1 tsp. fennel seeds
2 tsps. dried mint
2 tsps. salt
Olive oil
1 tsp. coriander seeds
1 tsp. freshly ground black pepper

1. Mix lamb, pistachios, eggs, lemon juice, chili flakes, flour, cumin seeds, fennel seeds, coriander seeds, mint, parsley, salt and black pepper in a large bowl.
2. Thread the lamb mixture onto metal skewers to form sausages and coat with olive oil.
3. Install a crisper plate in a basket. Place the skewers in the basket, then insert basket in unit.
4. Select Zone 1, select ROAST, set temperature to 355°F, and set time to 8 minutes. Press the START/PAUSE button to begin cooking.
5. With 4 minutes remaining, press START/PAUSE to pause the unit. Remove the basket from unit and flip the skewers over. Reinsert basket in unit and press START/PAUSE to resume cooking.
6. When cooking is complete, remove basket from unit. Transfer the skewers to a plate. Serve hot.

Fast Lamb Satay

PREP TIME: 5 minutes
COOK TIME: 10 minutes

¼ tsp. cumin
1 tsp. ginger
½ tsp. nutmeg
Salt and ground black pepper, to taste
2 boneless lamb steaks
Cooking spray

1. Combine the cumin, ginger, nutmeg, salt and pepper in a bowl.
2. Cube the lamb steaks and massage the spice mixture into each one.
3. Leave to marinate for 10 minutes, then transfer onto metal skewers.
4. Install a crisper plate in a basket. Place the skewers in the basket and spritz with the cooking spray, then insert basket in unit.
5. Select Zone 1, select AIR FRY, set temperature to 400°F, and set time to 10 minutes. Press the START/PAUSE button to begin cooking.
6. With 5 minutes remaining, press START/PAUSE to pause the unit. Remove the basket from unit and flip the skewers over. Reinsert basket in unit and press START/PAUSE to resume cooking.
7. When cooking is complete, remove basket from unit. Transfer skewers to a plate. Serve warm.

Smoky Beef Burgers

SERVES 4

PREP TIME: 20 minutes COOK TIME: 10 minutes	1 pound ground beef 4 whole-wheat hamburger buns, split and toasted 1 tbsp. Worcestershire sauce 1 tsp. Maggi seasoning sauce	3-4 drops liquid smoke 1 tsp. dried parsley ½ tsp. garlic powder ½ tsp. onion powder Salt and ground black pepper, as required

1. Mix the beef, sauces, liquid smoke, parsley, and spices in a bowl.
2. Make 4 equal-sized patties from the beef mixture.
3. Install a crisper plate in both baskets. Place 2 patties in a single layer in each basket.
4. Select Zone 1, select AIR FRY, set temperature to 350°F, and set time to 10 minutes. Select MATCH COOK to match Zone 2 settings to Zone 1. Select START/PAUSE to begin cooking.
5. When the Zone 1 and 2 times reach 5 minutes, press START/PAUSE to pause the unit. Remove the baskets from unit and flip the patties over. Reinsert baskets in unit and press START/PAUSE to resume cooking.
6. When cooking is complete, transfer patties to a plate. Serve warm.

Beef Cheeseburger Egg Rolls

MAKES 6 EGG ROLLS

PREP TIME: 15 minutes COOK TIME: 10 minutes	8 ounces (227 g) raw lean ground beef ½ cup chopped onion ½ cup chopped bell pepper ¼ tsp. onion powder ¼ tsp. garlic powder	3 tbsps. cream cheese 1 tbsp. yellow mustard 3 tbsps. shredded Cheddar cheese 6 chopped dill pickle chips 6 egg roll wrappers

1. In a skillet, add the beef, onion, bell pepper, onion powder, and garlic powder. Stir and crumble beef until fully cooked, and vegetables are soft.
2. Take skillet off the heat and add cream cheese, mustard, and Cheddar cheese, stirring until melted.
3. Pour beef mixture into a bowl and fold in pickles.
4. Lay out egg wrappers and divide the beef mixture into each one. Moisten egg roll wrapper edges with water. Fold sides to the middle and seal with water. Repeat with all other egg rolls.
5. Install a crisper plate in both baskets. Place half of the rolls in a single layer in each basket.
6. Select Zone 1, select AIR FRY, set temperature to 390°F, and set time to 10 minutes. Select MATCH COOK to match Zone 2 settings to Zone 1. Select START/PAUSE to begin cooking.
7. When cooking is complete, transfer the rolls to a plate. Serve hot.

Sweet Chicken Kabobs

SERVES 3

PREP TIME: 20 minutes COOK TIME: 10 minutes	4 scallions, chopped 2 tsps. sesame seeds, toasted 1 pound chicken tenders Wooden skewers, pres oaked 1 tbsp. fresh ginger, finely grated	4 garlic cloves, minced ½ cup pineapple juice ½ cup soy sauce ¼ cup sesame oil A pinch of black pepper

1. Mix scallion, ginger, garlic, pineapple juice, soy sauce, oil, sesame seeds, and black pepper in a large baking dish.
2. Thread chicken tenders onto pre-soaked wooden skewers.
3. Coat the skewers generously with marinade and refrigerate for about 2 hours.
4. Install a crisper plate in both baskets. Place half of the skewers in a single layer in each basket.
5. Select Zone 1, select ROAST, set temperature to 390°F, and set time to 10 minutes. Select MATCH COOK to match Zone 2 settings to Zone 1. Select START/PAUSE to begin cooking.
6. When the Zone 1 and 2 times reach 5 minutes, press START/PAUSE to pause the unit. Remove the baskets from unit and flip the skewers over. Reinsert baskets in unit and press START/PAUSE to resume cooking.
7. When cooking is complete, transfer skewers to a plate. Serve warm.

Beef and Veggie Kebabs

PREP TIME: 20 minutes
COOK TIME: 16 minutes

1 pound sirloin steak, cut into-inch chunks
8 ounces baby Bella mushrooms, stems removed
1 large bell pepper, seeded and cut into 1-inch pieces
1 red onion, cut into 1-inch pieces
¼ cup soy sauce
¼ cup olive oil
1 tbsp. garlic, minced
1 tsp. coconut sugar
½ tsp. ground cumin
Salt and black pepper, to taste

1. Mix soy sauce, oil, garlic, coconut sugar, cumin, salt, and black pepper in a large bowl.
2. Coat the steak cubes generously with marinade and refrigerate to marinate for about 30 minutes.
3. Thread the steak cubes, mushrooms, bell pepper, and onion onto metal skewers.
4. Install a crisper plate in both baskets. Place half of the skewers in a single layer in each basket.
5. Select Zone 1, select AIR FRY, set temperature to 390°F, and set time to 16 minutes. Select MATCH COOK to match Zone 2 settings to Zone 1. Select START/PAUSE to begin cooking.
6. When the Zone 1 and 2 times reach 8 minutes, press START/PAUSE to pause the unit. Remove the baskets from unit and flip the skewers over. Reinsert baskets in unit and press START/PAUSE to resume cooking.
7. When cooking is complete, transfer skewers to a plate. Serve warm.

Chicken and Veggie Kabobs

PREP TIME: 20 minutes
COOK TIME: 25 minutes

1 lb. skinless, boneless chicken thighs, cut into cubes
½ cup plain Greek yogurt
2 small tomatoes, seeded and cut into large chunks
1 large red onion, cut into large chunks
Wooden skewers, presoaked
1 tbsp. olive oil
2 tsps. curry powder
½ tsp. smoked paprika
¼ tsp. cayenne pepper
Salt, to taste

1. Mix the chicken, oil, yogurt, and spices in a large baking dish.
2. Thread chicken cubes, tomatoes and onion onto presoaked wooden skewers.
3. Coat the skewers generously with marinade and refrigerate for about 3 hours.
4. Install a crisper plate in both baskets. Place half of the skewers in each basket.
5. Select Zone 1, select ROAST, set temperature to 360°F, and set time to 25 minutes. Select MATCH COOK to match Zone 2 settings to Zone 1. Select START/PAUSE to begin cooking.
6. When the Zone 1 and 2 times reach 10 minutes, press START/PAUSE to pause the unit. Remove the baskets from unit and flip the skewers over. Reinsert baskets in unit and press START/PAUSE to resume cooking.
7. When cooking is complete, transfer skewers to a plate. Serve warm.

Chapter 6: Pork

Pork Loin with Potatoes

SERVES 5

PREP TIME: 15 minutes
COOK TIME: 30 minutes

2 pounds pork loin
1 tsp. fresh parsley, chopped
3 large red potatoes, chopped
3 tbsps. olive oil, divided
Salt and ground black pepper, as required
½ tsp. garlic powder
½ tsp. red pepper flakes, crushed

1. Rub the pork loin evenly with 1½ tbsps. olive oil, parsley, salt, and black pepper.
2. Mix the potatoes, remaining oil, garlic powder, red pepper flakes, salt, and black pepper in a bowl.
3. Install a crisper plate in both baskets. Place pork loin in the Zone 1 basket, then insert basket in unit. Place potatoes in the Zone 2 basket, then insert basket in unit.
4. Select Zone 1, select AIR FRY, set temperature to 390°F, and set time to 25 minutes. Select Zone 2, select AIR FRY, set temperature to 400°F, and set time to 30 minutes. Select SMART FINISH. Press the START/PAUSE button to begin cooking.
5. When the Zone 1 and Zone 2 times reach 10 minutes, press START/PAUSE and remove baskets from unit. In Zone 1, flip the pork loin over. In Zone 2, shake for 10 seconds. Reinsert baskets in unit and press START/PAUSE to resume cooking.
6. When cooking is complete, dish out in a bowl.
7. Cut pork loin into desired size slices and serve alongside potatoes.

Teriyaki Pork and Mushroom Rolls

SERVES 6

PREP TIME: 10 minutes
COOK TIME: 17 minutes

4 tbsps. brown sugar
4 tbsps. mirin
4 tbsps. soy sauce
1 tsp. almond flour
2-inch ginger, chopped
6 (4-ounce / 113-g) pork belly slices
6 ounces (170 g) Enoki mushrooms

1. Mix the brown sugar, mirin, soy sauce, almond flour, and ginger together until brown sugar dissolves.
2. Take pork belly slices and wrap around a bundle of mushrooms. Brush each roll with teriyaki sauce. Chill for half an hour.
3. Install a crisper plate in both baskets. Place 3 rolls in a single layer in each basket.
4. Select Zone 1, select AIR FRY, set temperature to 390°F, and set time to 17 minutes. Select MATCH COOK to match Zone 2 settings to Zone 1. Select START/PAUSE to begin cooking.
5. When the Zone 1 and 2 times reach 8 minutes, press START/PAUSE to pause the unit. Remove the baskets from unit and flip the rolls over. Reinsert baskets in unit and press START/PAUSE to resume cooking.
6. When cooking is complete, transfer rolls to a plate. Serve warm.

Pork Spare Ribs

PREP TIME: 15 minutes
COOK TIME: 22 minutes

12 (1-inch) pork spare ribs
½ cup cornstarch
5-6 garlic cloves, minced
½ cup rice vinegar
2 tbsps. soy sauce
2 tbsps. olive oil
Salt and black pepper, to taste

1. Mix the garlic, vinegar, soy sauce, salt, and black pepper in a large bowl.
2. Coat the ribs generously with this mixture and refrigerate to marinate overnight.
3. Place the cornstarch in a shallow bowl and dredge the ribs in it. Drizzle with olive oil.
4. Install a crisper plate in both baskets. Place half of ribs in a single layer in each basket.
5. Select Zone 1, select AIR FRY, set temperature to 390°F, and set time to 22 minutes. Select MATCH COOK to match Zone 2 settings to Zone 1. Select START/PAUSE to begin cooking.
6. When the Zone 1 and 2 times reach 10 minutes, press START/PAUSE to pause the unit. Remove the baskets from unit and flip the ribs over. Reinsert baskets in unit and press START/PAUSE to resume cooking.
7. When cooking is complete, transfer ribs to a plate. Serve warm.

Bacon Wrapped Pork Tenderloin

PREP TIME: 15 minutes
COOK TIME: 30 minutes

1 (1½ pound) pork tenderloin
4 bacon strips
2 tbsps. Dijon mustard

1. Rub the tenderloin evenly with mustard and wrap the tenderloin with bacon strips.
2. Install a crisper plate in a basket. Place pork tenderloin in the basket, then insert basket in unit.
3. Select Zone 1, select ROAST, set temperature to 390°F, and set time to 30 minutes. Press the START/PAUSE button to begin cooking.
4. With 15 minutes remaining, press START/PAUSE to pause the unit. Remove the basket from unit and flip the pork tenderloin over. Reinsert basket in unit and press START/PAUSE to resume cooking.
5. When cooking is complete, remove basket from unit. Transfer pork tenderloin to a plate. Cut into desired size slices to serve.

Sweet and Sour Pork Chops

PREP TIME: 10 minutes
COOK TIME: 20 minutes

6 pork loin chops
Salt and black pepper, to taste
2 garlic cloves, minced
2 tbsps. honey
2 tbsps. soy sauce
1 tbsp. balsamic vinegar
¼ tsp. ground ginger

1. Season the chops with a little salt and black pepper.
2. Mix rest of the ingredients in a large bowl and add chops.
3. Coat with marinade generously and cover to refrigerate for about 8 hours.
4. Install a crisper plate in both baskets. Place 3 chops in a single layer in each basket.
5. Select Zone 1, select AIR FRY, set temperature to 390°F, and set time to 20 minutes. Select MATCH COOK to match Zone 2 settings to Zone 1. Select START/PAUSE to begin cooking.
6. When the Zone 1 and 2 times reach 10 minutes, press START/PAUSE to pause the unit. Remove the baskets from unit and flip the chops over. Reinsert baskets in unit and press START/PAUSE to resume cooking.
7. When cooking is complete, transfer chops to a plate. Serve warm.

Chinese Pork Meatballs with Brussels Sprouts

PREP TIME: 15 minutes
COOK TIME: 22 minutes

For The Meatballs:
1 egg, beaten
6-ounce ground pork
¼ cup cornstarch
1 tsp. oyster sauce
½ tbsp. light soy sauce
½ tsp. sesame oil
¼ tsp. five spice powder

½ tbsp. olive oil
¼ tsp. honey
For the Brussels Sprouts:
2 cups Brussels sprouts, trimmed and halved lengthwise
1 tbsp. balsamic vinegar
1 tbsp. maple syrup
Salt, as required

1. Mix all the ingredients for Brussels Sprouts in a bowl and toss to coat well.
2. Mix all the ingredients for the meatballs in a bowl except cornstarch and oil until well combined.
3. Shape the mixture into equal-sized balls and place the cornstarch in a shallow dish.
4. Roll the meatballs evenly into cornstarch mixture.
5. Install a crisper plate in both baskets. Place Brussels Sprouts in the Zone 1 basket, then insert basket in unit. Place meatballs in the Zone 2 basket, then insert basket in unit.
6. Select Zone 1, select ROAST, set temperature to 400°F, and set time to 22 minutes. Select Zone 2, select AIR FRY, set temperature to 390°F, and set time to 16 minutes. Select SMART FINISH. Press the START/PAUSE button to begin cooking.
7. When the Zone 1 and Zone 2 times reach 8 minutes, press START/PAUSE and remove baskets from unit. In Zone 1, shake the Brussels Sprouts for 10 seconds. In Zone 2, flip the meatballs over. Reinsert baskets in unit and press START/PAUSE to resume cooking.
8. When cooking is complete, serve meatballs with Brussels Sprouts.

Potato and Prosciutto Salad

PREP TIME: 10 minutes COOK TIME: 35 minutes	For the Salad: 4 pounds (1.8 kg) potatoes, boiled and cubed 15 slices prosciutto, diced 2 cups shredded Cheddar cheese	For the Dressing: 15 ounces (425 g) sour cream 2 tbsps. mayonnaise 1 tsp. salt 1 tsp. black pepper 1 tsp. dried basil

1. Mix the potatoes, prosciutto, and Cheddar in a large bowl.
2. In a separate bowl, mix the sour cream, mayonnaise, salt, pepper, and basil using a whisk.
3. Install a crisper plate in both baskets. Place half of potato mixture in a single layer in each basket.
4. Select Zone 1, select AIR FRY, set temperature to 400°F, and set time to 35 minutes. Select MATCH COOK to match Zone 2 settings to Zone 1. Select START/PAUSE to begin cooking.
5. When the Zone 1 and 2 times reach 15 minutes, press START/PAUSE to pause the unit. Remove the baskets from unit and shake for 10 seconds. Reinsert baskets in unit and press START/PAUSE to resume cooking.
6. When cooking is complete, transfer salad to a plate. Serve warm with the dressing.

Filling Pork Chops

PREP TIME: 20 minutes COOK TIME: 15 minutes	2 (1-inch thick) pork chops ½ tbsp. fresh cilantro, chopped ½ tbsp. fresh rosemary, chopped ½ tbsp. fresh parsley, chopped 2 garlic cloves, minced	2 tbsps. olive oil ¾ tbsp. Dijon mustard 1 tbsp. ground coriander 1 tsp. coconut sugar Salt, to taste

1. Mix all the ingredients in a large bowl except the chops.
2. Coat the pork chops with marinade generously and cover to refrigerate for about 3 hours.
3. Keep the pork chops at room temperature for about 30 minutes.
4. Install a crisper plate in a basket. Place pork chops in the basket, then insert basket in unit.
5. Select Zone 1, select ROAST, set temperature to 390°F, and set time to 15 minutes. Press the START/PAUSE button to begin cooking.
6. With 7 minutes remaining, press START/PAUSE to pause the unit. Remove the basket from unit and flip the chops over. Reinsert basket in unit and press START/PAUSE to resume cooking.
7. When cooking is complete, remove basket from unit. Transfer chops to a plate. Serve warm.

Glazed Ham

PREP TIME: 10 minutes COOK TIME: 35 minutes	1 (1 pound) ham joint ¾ cup whiskey 2 tbsps. French mustard 2 tbsps. honey

1. Mix all the ingredients in a bowl except ham.
2. Keep ham joint for about 30 minutes at room temperature.
3. Install a crisper plate in a basket. Place ham joint in the basket and top with half of the whiskey mixture, then insert basket in unit.
4. Select Zone 1, select ROAST, set temperature to 390°F, and set time to 35 minutes. Press the START/PAUSE button to begin cooking.
5. With 15 minutes remaining, press START/PAUSE to pause the unit. Remove the basket from unit and flip the ham joint over. Coat with the remaining whiskey mixture. Reinsert basket in unit and press START/PAUSE to resume cooking.
6. When cooking is complete, remove basket from unit. Transfer ham joint to a plate. Serve warm.

Baked Chorizo Scotch Eggs

MAKES 4 EGGS

PREP TIME: 5 minutes
COOK TIME: 17 minutes

1 pound (454 g) Mexican chorizo or other seasoned sausage meat
4 soft-boiled eggs plus 1 raw egg
1 tbsp. water
½ cup all-purpose flour
1 cup panko bread crumbs
Cooking spray

1. Divide the chorizo into 4 equal portions. Flatten each portion into a disc. Place a soft-boiled egg in the center of each disc. Wrap the chorizo around the egg, encasing it completely. Place the encased eggs on a plate and chill for at least 30 minutes.
2. Beat the raw egg with 1 tbsp. of water. Place the flour on a small plate and the panko on a second plate. Working with 1 egg at a time, roll the encased egg in the flour, then dip it in the egg mixture. Dredge the egg in the panko and place on a plate. Repeat with the remaining eggs.
3. Install a crisper plate in both baskets. Spray the eggs with oil. Place 2 eggs in a single layer in each basket.
4. Select Zone 1, select BAKE, set temperature to 390°F, and set time to 17 minutes. Select MATCH COOK to match Zone 2 settings to Zone 1. Select START/PAUSE to begin cooking.
5. When the Zone 1 and 2 times reach 8 minutes, press START/PAUSE to pause the unit. Remove the baskets from unit and flip the eggs over. Reinsert baskets in unit and press START/PAUSE to resume cooking.
6. When cooking is complete, transfer eggs to a plate. Serve warm.

Breaded Pork Chops and Parsnips

SERVES 2

PREP TIME: 15 minutes
COOK TIME: 30 minutes

2 (6-ounces) pork chops
¼ cup plain flour
1 egg
4 ounces breadcrumbs
Salt and black pepper, to taste
1 tbsp. vegetable oil
10-ounces parsnips, peeled and cut into 1-inch chunks
1 tbsp. butter, melted

1. Mix parsnips and butter in a bowl and toss to coat well.
2. Season the chops with salt and black pepper.
3. Place the flour in a shallow bowl and whisk an egg in a second bowl.
4. Mix the breadcrumbs and vegetable oil in a third bowl.
5. Coat the pork chops with flour, dip into egg and dredge into the breadcrumb mixture.
6. Install a crisper plate in both baskets. Place parsnips in the Zone 1 basket, then insert basket in unit. Place chops in the Zone 2 basket, then insert basket in unit.
7. Select Zone 1, select AIR FRY, set temperature to 400°F, and set time to 30 minutes. Select Zone 2, select AIR FRY, set temperature to 390°F, and set time to 18 minutes. Select SMART FINISH. Press the START/PAUSE button to begin cooking.
8. When the Zone 1 and Zone 2 times reach 10 minutes, press START/PAUSE and remove baskets from unit. In Zone 1, shake for 10 seconds. In Zone 2, flip the pork chops over. Reinsert baskets in unit and press START/PAUSE to resume cooking.
9. When cooking is complete, serve chops with parsnips.

Chapter 7: Beef

Italian Beef Meatballs

SERVES 6

PREP TIME: 10 minutes
COOK TIME: 15 minutes

2 large eggs
2 pounds ground beef
¼ cup fresh parsley, chopped
1¼ cups panko breadcrumbs
¼ cup Parmigiano Reggiano, grated
1 tsp. dried oregano
1 small garlic clove, chopped
Salt and black pepper, to taste
1 tsp. vegetable oil

1. Mix beef with all other ingredients in a bowl until well combined. Make equal-sized balls from the mixture.
2. Install a crisper plate in both baskets. Place half of meatballs in a single layer in each basket.
3. Select Zone 1, select AIR FRY, set temperature to 360°F, and set time to 15 minutes. Select MATCH COOK to match Zone 2 settings to Zone 1. Select START/PAUSE to begin cooking.
4. When the Zone 1 and 2 times reach 7 minutes, press START/PAUSE to pause the unit. Remove the baskets from unit and flip the meatballs over. Reinsert baskets in unit and press START/PAUSE to resume cooking.
5. When cooking is complete, transfer meatballs to a plate. Serve warm.

Buttered Filet Mignon

SERVES 4

PREP TIME: 10 minutes
COOK TIME: 15 minutes

2 (6-ounces) filet mignon steaks
1 tbsp. butter, softened
Salt and black pepper, to taste

1. Rub the steak generously with salt and black pepper and coat with butter.
2. Install a crisper plate in a basket. Place the steaks in the basket, then insert basket in unit.
3. Select Zone 1, select ROAST, set temperature to 390°F, and set time to 15 minutes. Press the START/PAUSE button to begin cooking.
4. With 7 minutes remaining, press START/PAUSE to pause the unit. Remove the basket from unit and flip the steaks over. Reinsert basket in unit and press START/PAUSE to resume cooking.
5. When cooking is complete, remove basket from unit. Transfer the steaks to a plate and cut into desired size slices to serve.

Beef Jerky

SERVES 3

PREP TIME: 20 minutes
COOK TIME: 5 hours

1 pound bottom round beef, cut into thin strips
½ cup dark brown sugar
½ cup soy sauce
¼ cup Worcestershire sauce
1 tbsp. chili pepper sauce
1 tbsp. hickory liquid smoke
1 tsp. garlic powder
1 tsp. onion powder
1 tsp. cayenne pepper
½ tsp. smoked paprika
½ tsp. ground black pepper

1. Mix the brown sugar, all sauces, liquid smoke, and spices in a bowl.
2. Coat the beef strips with this marinade generously and marinate overnight.
3. Install a crisper plate in a basket. Place beef strips in the basket, then insert basket in unit.
4. Select Zone 1, select DEHYDRATE, set temperature to 150°F, and set time to 5 hours. Press the START/PAUSE button to begin cooking.
5. When cooking is complete, remove basket from unit. Transfer beef strips to a plate. Serve warm.

Tasty Beef Stuffed Bell Peppers

SERVES 4

PREP TIME: 20 minutes
COOK TIME: 30 minutes

½ medium onion, chopped
1 pound lean ground beef
½ cup jasmine rice, cooked
⅔ cup light Mexican cheese, shredded and divided
4 bell peppers, tops and seeds removed
1 tsp. olive oil
2 garlic cloves, minced
1 tsp. dried basil, crushed
1 tsp. garlic salt
½ tsp. red chili powder
Ground black pepper, as required
8 ounces tomato sauce, divided
2 tsps. Worcestershire sauce

1. Heat olive oil in a medium skillet over medium heat and add onion and garlic.
2. Sauté for about 5 minutes and add the ground beef, basil, and spices.
3. Cook for about 10 minutes and drain off the excess grease from skillet.
4. Stir in the rice, half of the cheese, ⅔ of the tomato sauce and Worcestershire sauce and mix well.
5. Stuff the beef mixture in each bell pepper.
6. Install a crisper plate in a basket. Place the bell peppers in the basket, then insert basket in unit.
7. Select Zone 1, select AIR FRY, set temperature to 390°F, and set time to 15 minutes. Press the START/PAUSE button to begin cooking.
8. With 10 minutes remaining, press START/PAUSE to pause the unit. Remove the basket from unit and top with the remaining tomato sauce and cheese. Reinsert basket in unit and press START/PAUSE to resume cooking.
9. When cooking is complete, remove basket from unit. Transfer bell peppers to a plate. Serve warm.

Herbed Beef Roast

PREP TIME: 10 minutes
COOK TIME: 45 minutes

2 pounds beef roast
1 tbsp. olive oil
1 tsp. dried rosemary, crushed
1 tsp. dried thyme, crushed
Salt, to taste

1. Rub the roast generously with herb mixture and coat with olive oil.
2. Install a crisper plate in a basket. Place the roast in the basket, then insert basket in unit.
3. Select Zone 1, select ROAST, set temperature to 390°F, and set time to 45 minutes. Press the START/PAUSE button to begin cooking.
4. With 20 minutes remaining, press START/PAUSE to pause the unit. Remove the basket from unit and flip the roast over. Reinsert basket in unit and press START/PAUSE to resume cooking.
5. When cooking is complete, remove basket from unit. Transfer the roast to a plate. Cut into desired size slices and serve.

Simple New York Strip Steak

PREP TIME: 10 minutes
COOK TIME: 16 minutes

1 (9½-ounces) New York strip steak
1 tsp. olive oil
Crushed red pepper flakes, to taste
Salt and black pepper, to taste

1. Rub the steak generously with red pepper flakes, salt and black pepper and coat with olive oil.
2. Install a crisper plate in a basket. Place the steak in the basket, then insert basket in unit.
3. Select Zone 1, select ROAST, set temperature to 390°F, and set time to 16 minutes. Press the START/PAUSE button to begin cooking.
4. With 8 minutes remaining, press START/PAUSE to pause the unit. Remove the basket from unit and flip the steak over. Reinsert basket in unit and press START/PAUSE to resume cooking.
5. When cooking is complete, remove basket from unit. Transfer the steak to a plate and cut into desired size slices to serve.

Holiday Spicy Beef Roast

SERVES 8

PREP TIME: 10 minutes **COOK TIME:** 40 minutes	2 pounds (907 g) roast beef, at room temperature 2 tbsps. extra-virgin olive oil 1 tsp. sea salt flakes 1 tsp. black pepper, preferably freshly ground 1 tsp. smoked paprika A few dashes of liquid smoke 2 jalapeño peppers, thinly sliced

1. Pat the roast dry using kitchen towels. Rub with extra-virgin olive oil and all seasonings along with liquid smoke.
2. Install a crisper plate in a basket. Place the roast in the basket, then insert basket in unit.
3. Select Zone 1, select AIR FRY, set temperature to 390°F, and set time to 40 minutes. Press the START/PAUSE button to begin cooking.
4. With 20 minutes remaining, press START/PAUSE to pause the unit. Remove the basket from unit and flip the roast over. Reinsert basket in unit and press START/PAUSE to resume cooking.
5. When cooking is complete, remove basket from unit. Transfer roast to a plate. Serve sprinkled with sliced jalapeños. Bon appétit!

Beef and Vegetable Cubes

SERVES 4

PREP TIME: 15 minutes **COOK TIME:** 18 minutes	2 tbsps. olive oil 1 tbsp. apple cider vinegar 1 tsp. fine sea salt ½ tsp. ground black pepper 1 tsp. shallot powder ¾ tsp. smoked cayenne pepper ½ tsp. garlic powder ¼ tsp. ground cumin 1 pound (454 g) top round steak, cut into cubes 4 ounces (113 g) broccoli, cut into florets 4 ounces (113 g) mushrooms, sliced 1 tsp. dried basil 1 tsp. celery seeds

1. Massage the olive oil, vinegar, salt, black pepper, shallot powder, cayenne pepper, garlic powder, and cumin into the cubed steak, ensuring to coat each piece evenly.
2. Allow to marinate for a minimum of 3 hours.
3. Install a crisper plate in both baskets. Place beef cubes in the Zone 1 basket, then insert basket in unit. Place vegetables in the Zone 2 basket along with basil and celery seeds, then insert basket in unit.
4. Select Zone 1, select AIR FRY, set temperature to 390°F, and set time to 12 minutes. Select Zone 2, select AIR FRY, set temperature to 390°F, and set time to 18 minutes. Select SMART FINISH. Press the START/PAUSE button to begin cooking.
5. When the Zone 1 and 2 times reach 6 minutes, press START/PAUSE to pause the unit. Remove the baskets from unit and shake for 10 seconds. Reinsert baskets in unit and press START/PAUSE to resume cooking.
6. When cooking is complete, serve beef cubes with vegetables.

Beef Tips with Onion

SERVES 2

PREP TIME: 15 minutes COOK TIME: 18 minutes	1 pound top round beef, cut into 1½-inch cubes ½ yellow onion, chopped 2 tbsps. Worcestershire sauce	1 tbsp. avocado oil 1 tsp. onion powder 1 tsp. garlic powder Salt and black pepper, to taste

1. Mix the beef tips, onion, Worcestershire sauce, avocado oil, and spices in a bowl.
2. Install a crisper plate in a basket. Place beef mixture in the basket, then insert basket in unit.
3. Select Zone 1, select AIR FRY, set temperature to 390°F, and set time to 18 minutes. Press the START/PAUSE button to begin cooking.
4. With 8 minutes remaining, press START/PAUSE to pause the unit. Remove the basket from unit and shake for 10 seconds. Reinsert basket in unit and press START/PAUSE to resume cooking.
5. When cooking is complete, remove basket from unit. Transfer beef mixture to a plate and cut into desired size slices to serve.

Crispy Sirloin Steak

SERVES 2

PREP TIME: 15 minutes COOK TIME: 18 minutes	1 cup white flour 2 eggs 1 cup panko breadcrumbs 2 (6-ounces) sirloin steaks, pounded	1 tsp. garlic powder 1 tsp. onion powder Salt and black pepper, to taste

1. Place the flour in a shallow bowl and whisk eggs in a second dish.
2. Mix the panko breadcrumbs and spices in a third bowl.
3. Rub the steaks with flour, dip into the eggs and coat with breadcrumb mixture.
4. Install a crisper plate in a basket. Place steaks in the basket, then insert basket in unit.
5. Select Zone 1, select AIR FRY, set temperature to 390°F, and set time to 18 minutes. Press the START/PAUSE button to begin cooking.
6. With 8 minutes remaining, press START/PAUSE to pause the unit. Remove the basket from unit and flip the steaks over. Reinsert basket in unit and press START/PAUSE to resume cooking.
7. When cooking is complete, remove basket from unit. Transfer steaks to a plate and cut into desired size slices to serve.

Air Fried London Broil

SERVES 8

PREP TIME: 15 minutes COOK TIME: 25 minutes	2 pounds (907 g) London broil 3 large garlic cloves, minced 3 tbsps. balsamic vinegar 3 tbsps. whole-grain mustard	2 tbsps. olive oil Sea salt and ground black pepper, to taste ½ tsp. dried hot red pepper flakes

1. Wash and dry the London broil. Score its sides with a knife.
2. Mix the remaining ingredients. Rub this mixture into the broil, coating it well. Allow to marinate for a minimum of 3 hours.
3. Install a crisper plate in a basket. Place the meat in the basket, then insert basket in unit.
4. Select Zone 1, select AIR FRY, set temperature to 400°F, and set time to 25 minutes. Press the START/PAUSE button to begin cooking.
5. With 10 minutes remaining, press START/PAUSE to pause the unit. Remove the basket from unit and flip the meat over. Reinsert basket in unit and press START/PAUSE to resume cooking.
6. When cooking is complete, remove basket from unit. Transfer London broil to a plate and cut into desired size slices to serve.

Chapter 8: Lamb

Lamb with Potatoes

SERVES 2

PREP TIME: 20 minutes
COOK TIME: 30 minutes

½ pound lamb meat
2 small potatoes, peeled and halved
½ small onion, peeled and halved
1 garlic clove, crushed
½ tbsp. dried rosemary, crushed
1 tsp. olive oil

1. Rub the lamb evenly with garlic and rosemary.
2. Add potatoes in a large bowl and stir in the olive oil and onions.
3. Install a crisper plate in both baskets. Place lamb in the Zone 1 basket, then insert basket in unit. Place vegetables in the Zone 2 basket, then insert basket in unit.
4. Select Zone 1, select ROAST, set temperature to 390°F, and set time to 25 minutes. Select Zone 2, select ROAST, set temperature to 400°F, and set time to 30 minutes. Select SMART FINISH. Press the START/PAUSE button to begin cooking.
5. When the Zone 1 and 2 times reach 15 minutes, press START/PAUSE to pause the unit. Remove the baskets from unit and flip the lamb and vegetables over. Reinsert baskets in unit and press START/PAUSE to resume cooking.
6. When cooking is complete, serve lamb with vegetables.

Leg of Lamb with Brussels Sprouts

SERVES 6

PREP TIME: 20 minutes
COOK TIME: 1 hour

2¼ pounds leg of lamb
1 tbsp. fresh rosemary, minced
1 tbsp. fresh lemon thyme
1½ pounds Brussels sprouts, trimmed
3 tbsps. olive oil, divided
1 garlic clove, minced
Salt and ground black pepper, as required
2 tbsps. honey

1. Make slits in the leg of lamb with a sharp knife.
2. Mix 2 tbsps. of oil, herbs, garlic, salt, and black pepper in a bowl.
3. Coat the leg of lamb with oil mixture generously.
4. Install a crisper plate in both baskets. Place leg of lamb in the Zone 1 basket, then insert basket in unit. Coat the Brussels sprouts evenly with the remaining oil and honey and arrange in the Zone 2 basket, then insert basket in unit.
5. Select Zone 1, select ROAST, set temperature to 400°F, and set time to 1 hour. Select Zone 2, select AIR FRY, set temperature to 400°F, and set time to 28 minutes. Select SMART FINISH. Press the START/PAUSE button to begin cooking.
6. When cooking is complete, serve lamb with vegetables.

Lamb Meatballs

PREP TIME: 20 minutes
COOK TIME: 27 minutes

For the Meatballs:
½ small onion, finely diced
1 clove garlic, minced
1 pound (454 g) ground lamb
2 tbsps. fresh parsley, finely
   chopped (plus more for garnish)
2 tsps. fresh oregano, finely chopped
2 tbsps. milk
1 egg yolk
Salt and freshly ground black pepper, to taste

½ cup crumbled feta cheese, for
   garnish
For the Tomato Sauce:
2 tbsps. butter
1 clove garlic, smashed
Pinch crushed red pepper flakes
¼ tsp. ground cinnamon
1 (28-ounce / 794-g) can crushed
   tomatoes
Salt, to taste
Cooking spray

1. Combine all ingredients for the meatballs in a large bowl and mix just until everything is combined. Shape the mixture into 1½-inch balls or shape the meat between two spoons to make quenelles.
2. Start the quick tomato sauce. Put the butter, garlic and red pepper flakes in a sauté pan and heat over medium heat on the stovetop. Let the garlic sizzle a little, but before the butter browns, add the cinnamon and tomatoes. Bring to a simmer and simmer for 15 minutes. Season with salt.
3. Install a crisper plate in both baskets. Place half of the meatballs in a single layer in each basket. Spray with cooking spray.
4. Select Zone 1, select AIR FRY, set temperature to 400°F, and set time to 12 minutes. Select MATCH COOK to match Zone 2 settings to Zone 1. Select START/PAUSE to begin cooking.
5. When the Zone 1 and 2 times reach 6 minutes, press START/PAUSE to pause the unit. Remove the baskets from unit and flip the meatballs over. Reinsert baskets in unit and press START/PAUSE to resume cooking.
6. When cooking is complete, transfer meatballs to a plate. To serve, spoon a pool of the tomato sauce onto plates and add the meatballs. Sprinkle the feta cheese on top and garnish with more fresh parsley. Serve immediately.

Fantastic Leg of Lamb

PREP TIME: 10 minutes
COOK TIME: 1 hour

2 pounds leg of lamb
2 fresh rosemary sprigs
2 fresh thyme sprigs
2 tbsps. olive oil
Salt and black pepper, to taste

1. Sprinkle the leg of lamb with oil, salt and black pepper and wrap with herb sprigs.
2. Install a crisper plate in a basket. Place leg of lamb in the basket, then insert basket in unit.
3. Select Zone 1, select ROAST, set temperature to 400°F, and set time to 50 minutes. Press the START/PAUSE button to begin cooking.
4. With 25 minutes remaining, press START/PAUSE to pause the unit. Remove the basket from unit and flip the leg of lamb over. Reinsert basket in unit and press START/PAUSE to resume cooking.
5. When cooking is complete, remove basket from unit. Transfer leg of lamb to a plate. Serve warm.

Simple Lamb Chops

SERVES 2

PREP TIME: 10 minutes
COOK TIME: 15 minutes

4 (4-ounces) lamb chops
Salt and black pepper, to taste
1 tbsp. olive oil

1. Mix the olive oil, salt, and black pepper in a large bowl and add chops.
2. Install a crisper plate in a basket. Place the chops in the basket, then insert basket in unit.
3. Select Zone 1, select AIR FRY, set temperature to 390°F, and set time to 15 minutes. Press the START/PAUSE button to begin cooking.
4. With 7 minutes remaining, press START/PAUSE to pause the unit. Remove the basket from unit and flip the chops over. Reinsert basket in unit and press START/PAUSE to resume cooking.
5. When cooking is complete, remove basket from unit. Transfer the chops to a plate. Serve warm.

Air Fried Lamb Ribs

SERVES 4

PREP TIME: 5 minutes
COOK TIME: 18 minutes

2 tbsps. mustard
1 pound (454 g) lamb ribs
1 tsp. rosemary, chopped
Salt and ground black pepper, to taste
¼ cup mint leaves, chopped
1 cup Green yogurt

1. Use a brush to apply the mustard to the lamb ribs, and season with rosemary, salt, and pepper.
2. Install a crisper plate in a basket. Place lamb ribs in the basket, then insert basket in unit.
3. Select Zone 1, select AIR FRY, set temperature to 390°F, and set time to 18 minutes. Press the START/PAUSE button to begin cooking.
4. With 9 minutes remaining, press START/PAUSE to pause the unit. Remove the basket from unit and flip the lamb ribs over. Reinsert basket in unit and press START/PAUSE to resume cooking.
5. Meanwhile, combine the mint leaves and yogurt in a bowl.
6. When cooking is complete, remove basket from unit. Transfer lamb ribs to a plate and serve with the mint yogurt.

Mustard Lamb Loin Chops

PREP TIME: 15 minutes COOK TIME: 18 minutes	8 (4-ounces) lamb loin chops 2 tbsps. Dijon mustard 1 tbsp. fresh lemon juice ½ tsp. olive oil 1 tsp. dried tarragon Salt and black pepper, to taste

1. Mix the mustard, lemon juice, oil, tarragon, salt, and black pepper in a large bowl.
2. Coat the chops generously with the mustard mixture.
3. Install a crisper plate in both baskets. Place 4 chops in a single layer in each basket.
4. Select Zone 1, select ROAST, set temperature to 390°F, and set time to 18 minutes. Select MATCH COOK to match Zone 2 settings to Zone 1. Select START/PAUSE to begin cooking.
5. When the Zone 1 and 2 times reach 8 minutes, press START/PAUSE to pause the unit. Remove the baskets from unit and flip the chops over. Reinsert baskets in unit and press START/PAUSE to resume cooking.
6. When cooking is complete, transfer chops to a plate. Serve warm.

Spiced Lamb Steaks

PREP TIME: 15 minutes COOK TIME: 15 minutes	½ onion, roughly chopped 1½ pounds boneless lamb sirloin steaks 5 garlic cloves, peeled 1 tbsp. fresh ginger, peeled 1 tsp. garam masala	1 tsp. ground fennel ½ tsp. ground cumin ½ tsp. ground cinnamon ½ tsp. cayenne pepper Salt and black pepper, to taste

1. Put the onion, garlic, ginger, and spices in a blender and pulse until smooth.
2. Coat the lamb steaks with this mixture on both sides and refrigerate to marinate for about 24 hours.
3. Install a crisper plate in a basket. Place lamb steaks in the basket, then insert basket in unit.
4. Select Zone 1, select ROAST, set temperature to 390°F, and set time to 15 minutes. Press the START/PAUSE button to begin cooking.
5. With 8 minutes remaining, press START/PAUSE to pause the unit. Remove the basket from unit and flip the lamb steaks over. Reinsert basket in unit and press START/PAUSE to resume cooking.
6. When cooking is complete, remove basket from unit. Transfer lamb steaks to a plate. Serve warm.

Italian Lamb Chops with Avocado Mayo

PREP TIME: 5 minutes COOK TIME: 12 minutes	2 lamp chops 2 tsps. Italian herbs 2 avocados ½ cup mayonnaise 1 tbsp. lemon juice

1. Season the lamb chops with the Italian herbs, then set aside for 5 minutes.
2. Install a crisper plate in a basket. Place lamb chops in the basket, then insert basket in unit.
3. Select Zone 1, select AIR FRY, set temperature to 400°F, and set time to 12 minutes. Press the START/PAUSE button to begin cooking.
4. With 6 minutes remaining, press START/PAUSE to pause the unit. Remove the basket from unit and flip the lamb chops over. Reinsert basket in unit and press START/PAUSE to resume cooking.
5. In the meantime, halve the avocados and open to remove the pits. Spoon the flesh into a blender.
6. Add the mayonnaise and lemon juice and pulse until a smooth consistency is achieved.
7. When cooking is complete, remove basket from unit. Transfer lamb chops to a plate. Serve warm with the avocado mayo.

Pesto Coated Rack of Lamb

SERVES 4

PREP TIME: 15 minutes COOK TIME: 18 minutes	½ bunch fresh mint 1 (1½-pounds) rack of lamb 1 garlic clove ¼ cup extra-virgin olive oil ½ tbsp. honey Salt and black pepper, to taste

1. Put the mint, garlic, oil, honey, salt, and black pepper in a blender and pulse until smooth to make pesto.
2. Coat the rack of lamb with this pesto on both sides.
3. Install a crisper plate in a basket. Place the rack of lamb in the basket, then insert basket in unit.
4. Select Zone 1, select ROAST, set temperature to 390°F, and set time to 18 minutes. Press the START/PAUSE button to begin cooking.
5. With 8 minutes remaining, press START/PAUSE to pause the unit. Remove the basket from unit and flip the rack of lamb over. Reinsert basket in unit and press START/PAUSE to resume cooking.
6. When cooking is complete, remove basket from unit. Transfer the rack of lamb to a plate and cut the rack into individual chops to serve.

Scrumptious Lamb Chops

SERVES 4

PREP TIME: 20 minutes COOK TIME: 18 minutes	2 tbsps. fresh mint leaves, minced 4 (6-ounce) lamb chops 2 carrots, peeled and cubed 1 parsnip, peeled and cubed 1 fennel bulb, cubed 1 garlic clove, minced 2 tbsps. dried rosemary 3 tbsps. olive oil Salt and black pepper, to taste

1. Mix herbs, garlic and oil in a large bowl and coat lamp chops generously with this mixture.
2. Marinate in the refrigerator for about 3 hours.
3. Soak the vegetables in a large pan of water for about 15 minutes.
4. Install a crisper plate in both baskets. Place lamp chops in the Zone 1 basket, then insert basket in unit. Place vegetables in the Zone 2 basket, then insert basket in unit.
5. Select Zone 1, select ROAST, set temperature to 390°F, and set time to 18 minutes. Select Zone 2, select ROAST, set temperature to 390°F, and set time to 10 minutes. Select SMART FINISH. Press the START/PAUSE button to begin cooking.
6. When the Zone 1 and 2 times reach 6 minutes, press START/PAUSE to pause the unit. Remove the baskets from unit and flip the lamp chops and vegetables over. Reinsert baskets in unit and press START/PAUSE to resume cooking.
7. When cooking is complete, serve lamp chops with vegetables.

Chapter 9: Bread and Cake

Chocolate Molten Cake

SERVES 4

PREP TIME: 5 minutes
COOK TIME: 12 minutes

3.5 ounces (99 g) butter, melted
3½ tbsps. sugar
3.5 ounces (99 g) chocolate, melted
1½ tbsps. flour
2 eggs

1. Grease four 3-inch ramekins with a little butter.
2. Rigorously combine the eggs, butter, and sugar before stirring in the melted chocolate.
3. Slowly fold in the flour.
4. Spoon an equal amount of the mixture into each ramekin.
5. Install a crisper plate in both baskets. Place 2 ramekins in each basket.
6. Select Zone 1, select BAKE, set temperature to 375°F, and set time to 12 minutes. Select MATCH COOK to match Zone 2 settings to Zone 1. Select START/PAUSE to begin cooking.
7. When cooking is complete, put the ramekins upside-down on plates and let the cakes fall out. Serve hot.

Nutty Zucchini Bread

SERVES 6

PREP TIME: 15 minutes
COOK TIME: 20 minutes

3 cups all-purpose flour
2 tsps. baking powder
3 eggs
2 cups zucchini, grated
1 cup walnuts, chopped
1 tbsp. ground cinnamon
1 tsp. salt
2¼ cups white sugar
1 cup vegetable oil
3 tsps. vanilla extract

1. Grease two (7x4-inch) loaf pans.
2. Mix together the flour, baking powder, cinnamon and salt in a bowl.
3. Whisk together eggs with sugar, vanilla extract and vegetable oil in a bowl until combined.
4. Stir in the flour mixture and fold in the zucchini and walnuts.
5. Mix until combined and transfer the mixture into the prepared loaf pans.
6. Install a crisper plate in both baskets. Place 1 loaf pan in each basket.
7. Select Zone 1, select BAKE, set temperature to 320°F, and set time to 20 minutes. Select MATCH COOK to match Zone 2 settings to Zone 1. Select START/PAUSE to begin cooking.
8. When cooking is complete, remove from the Air fryer and place onto a wire rack to cool.
9. Cut the bread into desired size slices and serve.

Banana Bread

PREP TIME: 10 minutes
COOK TIME: 22 minutes

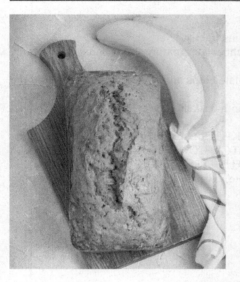

2 ripe bananas, mashed
1 cup sugar
1 large egg
4 tbsps. (½ stick) unsalted butter, melted
1 cup all-purpose flour
1 tsp. baking soda
1 tsp. salt

1. Coat the insides of 2 mini loaf pans with cooking spray.
2. In a large mixing bowl, mix the bananas and sugar.
3. In a separate large mixing bowl, combine the egg, butter, flour, baking soda, and salt and mix well.
4. Add the banana mixture to the egg and flour mixture. Mix well.
5. Divide the batter evenly among the prepared pans.
6. Install a crisper plate in both baskets. Place 1 loaf pan in each basket.
7. Select Zone 1, select BAKE, set temperature to 350°F, and set time to 22 minutes. Select MATCH COOK to match Zone 2 settings to Zone 1. Select START/PAUSE to begin cooking. Insert a toothpick into the center of each loaf; if it comes out clean, they are done.
8. When the loaves are cooked through, remove the pans from the air fryer basket. Turn out the loaves onto a wire rack to cool.
9. Serve warm.

Sunflower Seeds Bread

PREP TIME: 15 minutes
COOK TIME: 18 minutes

⅔ cup whole wheat flour
⅔ cup plain flour
⅓ cup sunflower seeds
1 cup lukewarm water
½ sachet instant yeast
1 tsp. salt

1. Grease a 7 x 4-inch cake pan.
2. Mix together flours, sunflower seeds, yeast and salt in a bowl.
3. Add water slowly and knead for about 5 minutes until a dough is formed.
4. Cover the dough with a plastic wrap and keep in warm place for about half an hour.
5. Arrange the dough into the cake pan.
6. Install a crisper plate in a basket. Place the cake pan in the basket, then insert basket in unit.
7. Select Zone 1, select BAKE, set temperature to 390°F, and set time to 18 minutes. Press the START/PAUSE button to begin cooking.
8. When cooking is complete, remove basket from unit. Serve warm.

Heavenly Tasty Lava Cake

SERVES 4

PREP TIME: 10 minutes
COOK TIME: 6 minutes

⅔ cup unsalted butter
2 eggs
⅔ cup all-purpose flour
1 cup chocolate chips, melted
⅓ cup fresh raspberries
5 tbsps. sugar
Salt, to taste

1. Grease four 3-inch ramekins lightly.
2. Mix sugar, butter, eggs, chocolate mixture, flour and salt in a bowl until well combined.
3. Fold in the melted chocolate chips and divide this mixture into the prepared ramekins.
4. Install a crisper plate in both baskets. Place 2 ramekins in each basket.
5. Select Zone 1, select BAKE, set temperature to 355°F, and set time to 6 minutes. Select MATCH COOK to match Zone 2 settings to Zone 1. Select START/PAUSE to begin cooking.
6. When cooking is complete, garnish with raspberries and serve immediately.

Simple Apple Cake

SERVES 6

PREP TIME: 10 minutes
COOK TIME: 45 minutes

1 cup all-purpose flour
½ tsp. baking soda
1 egg
2 cups apples, peeled, cored and chopped
⅓ cup brown sugar
1 tsp. ground nutmeg
1 tsp. ground cinnamon
Salt, to taste
5 tbsps. plus 1 tsp. vegetable oil
¾ tsp. vanilla extract

1. Grease a 7 x 5-inch baking pan lightly.
2. Mix flour, sugar, spices, baking soda and salt in a bowl until well combined.
3. Whisk egg with oil and vanilla extract in another bowl.
4. Stir in the flour mixture slowly and fold in the apples.
5. Pour this mixture into the baking pan and cover with the foil paper.
6. Install a crisper plate in a basket. Place the baking pan in the basket, then insert basket in unit.
7. Select Zone 1, select BAKE, set temperature to 355°F, and set time to 45 minutes. Press the START/PAUSE button to begin cooking.
8. With 5 minutes remaining, press START/PAUSE to pause the unit. Remove the basket from unit and remove the foil. Reinsert basket in unit and press START/PAUSE to resume cooking.
9. When cooking is complete, remove basket from unit. Allow to cool completely and cut into slices to serve.

English Pumpkin Egg Cake

SERVES 2

PREP TIME: 10 minutes		
COOK TIME: 10 minutes	2 eggs	1 tbsp. sugar
	½ cup milk	1 cup pumpkin purée
	2 cups flour	1 tsp. cinnamon powder
	2 tbsps. cider vinegar	1 tsp. baking soda
	2 tsps. baking powder	1 tbsp. olive oil

1. Crack the eggs into a bowl and beat with a whisk. Combine with the milk, flour, cider vinegar, baking powder, sugar, pumpkin purée, cinnamon powder, and baking soda, mixing well.
2. Grease a 7 x 5-inch baking dish with oil.
3. Install a crisper plate in a basket. Add the mixture in the baking dish and arrange in the basket, then insert basket in unit.
4. Select Zone 1, select BAKE, set temperature to 300°F, and set time to 10 minutes. Press the START/PAUSE button to begin cooking.
5. When cooking is complete, serve warm.

Cream Bread

SERVES 8

PREP TIME: 20 minutes		
COOK TIME: 50 minutes	1 cup milk	¾ cup whipping cream
	1 large egg	1 tsp. salt
	3½ cups bread flour	¼ cup fine sugar
	½ cup all-purpose flour	3 tsps. dry yeast
	2 tbsps. milk powder	

1. Grease two 7 x 4-inch cake pans.
2. Mix together all the dry ingredients with the wet ingredients to form a dough.
3. Divide the dough into 4 equal-sized balls and roll each ball into a rectangle.
4. Roll each rectangle like a Swiss roll tightly and place 2 rolls into each prepared cake pan. Keep aside for about 1 hour.
5. Install a crisper plate in both baskets. Place one cake pan in each basket.
6. Select Zone 1, select BAKE, set temperature to 375°F, and set time to 50 minutes. Select MATCH COOK to match Zone 2 settings to Zone 1. Select START/PAUSE to begin cooking.
7. When cooking is complete, remove the bread rolls from pans.
8. Cut each roll into desired size slices and serve warm.

Decadent Cheesecake

SERVES 6

PREP TIME: 15 minutes		
COOK TIME: 33 minutes	3 eggs, separated	2 tbsps. cocoa powder
	1 cup white chocolate, chopped	¼ cup apricot jam
	½ cup cream cheese, softened	2 tbsps. powdered sugar

1. Grease a 7 x 4-inch cake pan lightly.
2. Refrigerate egg whites in a bowl to chill before using.
3. Microwave chocolate and cream cheese on high for about 3 minutes.
4. Remove from microwave and whisk in the egg yolks.
5. Whisk together egg whites until firm peaks form and combine with the chocolate mixture. Transfer the mixture into the cake pan.
6. Install a crisper plate in a basket. Place the cake pan in the basket, then insert basket in unit.
7. Select Zone 1, select BAKE, set temperature to 285°F, and set time to 30 minutes. Press the START/PAUSE button to begin cooking.
8. When cooking is complete, remove basket from unit. Dust with powdered sugar and spread jam on top to serve.

Bourbon Monkey Bread

SERVES 6

PREP TIME: 15 minutes COOK TIME: 25 minutes	1 (16.3-ounce / 462-g) can store-bought refrigerated biscuit dough ¼ cup packed light brown sugar 1 tsp. ground cinnamon ½ tsp. freshly grated nutmeg ½ tsp. ground ginger ½ tsp. kosher salt ¼ tsp. ground allspice ⅛ tsp. ground cloves 4 tbsps. (½ stick) unsalted butter, melted ½ cup powdered sugar 2 tsps. bourbon 2 tbsps. chopped candied cherries 2 tbsps. chopped pecans

1. Open the can and separate the biscuits, then cut each into quarters. Toss the biscuit quarters in a large bowl with the brown sugar, cinnamon, nutmeg, ginger, salt, allspice, and cloves until evenly coated. Transfer the dough pieces and any sugar left in the bowl into a 5-inch round cake pan and drizzle evenly with the melted butter.
2. Install a crisper plate in a basket. Place cake pan in the basket, then insert basket in unit.
3. Select Zone 1, select BAKE, set temperature to 310°F, and set time to 25 minutes. Press the START/PAUSE button to begin cooking, until the monkey bread is golden brown and cooked through in the middle.
4. When cooking is complete, remove basket from unit. Transfer the pan to a wire rack and let cool completely. Un-mold from the pan.
5. In a small bowl, whisk the powdered sugar and the bourbon into a smooth glaze. Drizzle the glaze over the cooled monkey bread and, while the glaze is still wet, sprinkle with the cherries and pecans to serve.

Eggnog Bread

SERVES 6

PREP TIME: 10 minutes COOK TIME: 18 minutes	1 cup flour, plus more for dusting ¼ cup sugar 1 tsp. baking powder ¼ tsp. salt ¼ tsp. nutmeg ½ cup eggnog 1 egg yolk 1 tbsp. plus 1 tsp. butter, melted ¼ cup pecans ¼ cup chopped candied fruit (cherries, pineapple, or mixed fruits) Cooking spray

1. In a medium bowl, stir together the flour, sugar, baking powder, salt, and nutmeg.
2. Add the eggnog, egg yolk, and butter. Mix well but do not beat.
3. Stir in nuts and fruit.
4. Spray a 7 x 5-inch baking pan with cooking spray and dust with flour. Spread batter into the prepared pan.
5. Install a crisper plate in a basket. Place the baking pan in the basket, then insert basket in unit.
6. Select Zone 1, select BAKE, set temperature to 360°F, and set time to 18 minutes. Press the START/PAUSE button to begin cooking, until top is dark golden brown and bread starts to pull away from sides of pan.
7. When cooking is complete, serve immediately.

Chapter 10: Snack

Rosemary Baked Cashews

MAKES 2 CUPS

PREP TIME: 5 minutes
COOK TIME: 5 minutes

2 sprigs of fresh rosemary (1 chopped and 1 whole)
1 tsp. olive oil
1 tsp. kosher salt
½ tsp. honey
2 cups roasted and unsalted whole cashews
Cooking spray

1. In a medium bowl, whisk together the chopped rosemary, olive oil, kosher salt, and honey. Set aside.
2. Install a crisper plate in a basket and spray with cooking spray. Place the cashews and the whole rosemary sprig in the basket, then insert basket in unit.
3. Select Zone 1, select BAKE, set temperature to 300°F, and set time to 5 minutes. Press the START/PAUSE button to begin cooking.
4. When cooking is complete, remove cashews and rosemary from unit, then discard the rosemary and add the cashews to the olive oil mixture, tossing to coat.
5. Allow to cool for 15 minutes before serving.

Air Fried Pot Stickers

MAKES 30 POT STICKERS

PREP TIME: 10 minutes
COOK TIME: 12 minutes

½ cup finely chopped cabbage
¼ cup finely chopped red bell pepper
2 green onions, finely chopped
1 egg, beaten
2 tbsps. cocktail sauce
2 tsps. low-sodium soy sauce
30 wonton wrappers
1 tbsp. water, for brushing the wrappers

1. In a small bowl, combine the cabbage, pepper, green onions, egg, cocktail sauce, and soy sauce, and mix well.
2. Put about 1 tsp. of the mixture in the center of each wonton wrapper. Fold the wrapper in half, covering the filling; dampen the edges with water, and seal. You can crimp the edges of the wrapper with your fingers so they look like the pot stickers you get in restaurants. Brush them with water.
3. Install a crisper plate in both baskets. Place half of the pot stickers in each basket.
4. Select Zone 1, select AIR FRY, set temperature to 360°F, and set time to 12 minutes. Select MATCH COOK to match Zone 2 settings to Zone 1. Select START/PAUSE to begin cooking, until the pot stickers are hot and the bottoms are lightly browned.
5. Serve hot.

Lemony Pear Chips

SERVES 4

PREP TIME: 15 minutes
COOK TIME: 10 minutes

2 firm Bosc pears, cut crosswise into ⅛-inch-thick slices
1 tbsp. freshly squeezed lemon juice
½ tsp. ground cinnamon
⅛ tsp. ground cardamom

1. Separate the smaller stem-end pear rounds from the larger rounds with seeds. Remove the core and seeds from the larger slices. Sprinkle all slices with lemon juice, cinnamon, and cardamom.
2. Install a crisper plate in both baskets. Place half of the chips in each basket.
3. Select Zone 1, select AIR FRY, set temperature to 380°F, and set time to 10 minutes. Select MATCH COOK to match Zone 2 settings to Zone 1. Select START/PAUSE to begin cooking.
4. When the Zone 1 and 2 times reach 5 minutes, press START/PAUSE to pause the unit. Remove the baskets from unit and shake for 10 seconds. Reinsert baskets in unit and press START/PAUSE to resume cooking.
5. When cooking is complete, remove basket from unit. Cool and serve or store in an airtight container at room temperature up for to 2 days.

Coconut-Crusted Shrimp

SERVES 2 TO 4

PREP TIME: 10 minutes
COOK TIME: 7 minutes

½ pound (227 g) medium shrimp, peeled and deveined (tails intact)
1 cup canned coconut milk
Finely grated zest of 1 lime
Kosher salt, to taste
½ cup panko bread crumbs

½ cup unsweetened shredded coconut
Freshly ground black pepper, to taste
Cooking spray
1 small or ½ medium cucumber, halved and deseeded
1 cup coconut yogurt
1 serrano chile, deseeded and minced

1. In a bowl, combine the shrimp, coconut milk, lime zest, and ½ tsp. kosher salt. Let the shrimp stand for 10 minutes.
2. Meanwhile, in a separate bowl, stir together the bread crumbs and shredded coconut and season with salt and pepper.
3. A few at a time, add the shrimp to the bread crumb mixture and toss to coat completely. Transfer the shrimp to a wire rack set over a baking sheet. Spray the shrimp all over with cooking spray.
4. Install a crisper plate in a basket. Place the shrimp in the basket, then insert basket in unit.
5. Select Zone 1, select AIR FRY, set temperature to 390°F, and set time to 7 minutes. Press the START/PAUSE button to begin cooking.
6. When cooking is complete, remove basket from unit. Transfer the shrimp to a serving platter and season with more salt.
7. Grate the cucumber into a small bowl. Stir in the coconut yogurt and chile and season with salt and pepper. Serve alongside the shrimp while they're warm.

Peppery Chicken Meatballs

PREP TIME: 5 minutes
COOK TIME: 18 to 20 minutes

2 tsps. olive oil
¼ cup minced onion
¼ cup minced red bell pepper
2 vanilla wafers, crushed
1 egg white
½ tsp. dried thyme
½ pound (227 g) ground chicken breast

1. In a skillet over medium heat, add the olive oil, onion, and red bell pepper. Cook for 3 to 5 minutes, until the vegetables are tender.
2. In a medium bowl, mix the cooked vegetables, crushed wafers, egg white, and thyme until well combined
3. Mix in the chicken, gently but thoroughly, until everything is combined. Form the mixture into 16 meatballs.
4. Install a crisper plate in both baskets. Place 8 meatballs in a single layer in each basket.
5. Select Zone 1, select AIR FRY, set temperature to 370°F, and set time to 15 minutes. Select MATCH COOK to match Zone 2 settings to Zone 1. Select START/PAUSE to begin cooking.
6. When the Zone 1 and 2 times reach 8 minutes, press START/PAUSE to pause the unit. Remove the baskets from unit and flip the meatballs over. Reinsert baskets in unit and press START/PAUSE to resume cooking.
7. When cooking is complete, transfer meatballs to a plate. Serve warm.

Rosemary-Garlic Shoestring Fries

PREP TIME: 5 minutes
COOK TIME: 18 minutes

1 large russet potato (about 12 ounces / 340 g), scrubbed clean, and julienned
1 tbsp. vegetable oil
Leaves from 1 sprig fresh rosemary
Kosher salt and freshly ground black pepper, to taste
1 garlic clove, thinly sliced
Flaky sea salt, for serving

1. Place the julienned potatoes in a large colander and rinse under cold running water until the water runs clear. Spread the potatoes out on a double-thick layer of paper towels and pat dry.
2. In a large bowl, combine the potatoes, oil, and rosemary. Season with kosher salt and pepper and toss to coat evenly.
3. Install a crisper plate in a basket. Place potatoes in the basket, then insert basket in unit.
4. Select Zone 1, select AIR FRY, set temperature to 400°F, and set time to 18 minutes. Press the START/PAUSE button to begin cooking.
5. With 10 minutes remaining, press START/PAUSE to pause the unit. Remove the basket from unit and shake for 10 seconds. Reinsert basket in unit and press START/PAUSE to resume cooking.
6. With 5 minutes remaining, press START/PAUSE to pause the unit. Remove the basket from unit. Shake for 10 seconds and add the garlic. Reinsert basket in unit and press START/PAUSE to resume cooking.
7. When cooking is complete, remove basket from unit. Transfer fries to a plate and sprinkle with flaky sea salt while they're hot. Serve immediately.

Cheesy Steak Fries

SERVES 5

PREP TIME: 5 minutes COOK TIME: 20 minutes	1 (28-ounce / 794-g) bag frozen steak fries Cooking spray Salt and pepper, to taste ½ cup beef gravy 1 cup shredded Mozzarella cheese 2 scallions, green parts only, chopped

1. Install a crisper plate in a basket. Place frozen steak fries in the basket, then insert basket in unit.
2. Select Zone 1, select AIR FRY, set temperature to 400°F, and set time to 20 minutes. Press the START/PAUSE button to begin cooking.
3. With 10 minutes remaining, press START/PAUSE to pause the unit. Remove the basket from unit. Shake for 10 seconds and spritz the fries with cooking spray. Reinsert basket in unit and press START/PAUSE to resume cooking.
4. Meanwhile, pour the beef gravy into a medium, microwave-safe bowl. Microwave for 30 seconds, or until the gravy is warm.
5. With 2 minutes remaining, press START/PAUSE to pause the unit. Remove the basket from unit. Sprinkle the fries with the cheese. Reinsert basket in unit and press START/PAUSE to resume cooking, until the cheese is melted.
6. When cooking is complete, remove basket from unit. Transfer the fries to a serving dish. Drizzle the fries with gravy and sprinkle the scallions on top for a green garnish. Serve.

Air Fried Spicy Olives

SERVES 4

PREP TIME: 10 minutes COOK TIME: 6 minutes	12 ounces (340 g) extra-large pitted black olives ¼ cup all-purpose flour 1 cup panko bread crumbs 2 tsps. dried thyme 1 tsp. red pepper flakes 1 tsp. smoked paprika 1 egg beaten with 1 tbsp. water Vegetable oil for spraying

1. Drain the olives and place them on a paper towel–lined plate to dry.
2. Put the flour on a plate. Combine the panko, thyme, red pepper flakes, and paprika on a separate plate. Dip an olive in the flour, shaking off any excess, then coat with egg mixture. Dredge the olive in the panko mixture, pressing to make the crumbs adhere, and place the breaded olives on a platter. Repeat with the remaining olives.
3. Install a crisper plate in a basket. Place olives in the basket, then insert basket in unit.
4. Select Zone 1, select AIR FRY, set temperature to 400°F, and set time to 6 minutes. Press the START/PAUSE button to begin cooking.
5. With 3 minutes remaining, press START/PAUSE to pause the unit. Remove the basket from unit and flip the olives over. Reinsert basket in unit and press START/PAUSE to resume cooking, until the breading is browned and crispy.
6. When cooking is complete, remove basket from unit. Serve warm.

Cheesy Hash Brown Bruschetta

PREP TIME: 5 minutes	4 frozen hash brown patties	2 tbsps. grated Parmesan cheese
COOK TIME: 10 minutes	1 tbsp. olive oil	1 tbsp. balsamic vinegar
	⅓ cup chopped cherry tomatoes	1 tbsp. minced fresh basil
	3 tbsps. diced fresh Mozzarella	

1. Install a crisper plate in both baskets. Place 2 hash brown patties in a single layer in each basket.
2. Select Zone 1, select AIR FRY, set temperature to 400°F, and set time to 10 minutes. Select MATCH COOK to match Zone 2 settings to Zone 1. Select START/PAUSE to begin cooking, until the potatoes are crisp, hot, and golden brown.
3. Meanwhile, combine the olive oil, tomatoes, Mozzarella, Parmesan, vinegar, and basil in a small bowl.
4. When cooking is complete, transfer hash brown patties to a serving plate. Top with the tomato mixture and serve.

Spiced Mixed Nuts

PREP TIME: 5 minutes	½ cup raw cashews	1 tsp. chopped fresh thyme leaves
COOK TIME: 6 minutes	½ cup raw pecan halves	1 tsp. kosher salt
	½ cup raw walnut halves	½ tsp. ground coriander
	½ cup raw whole almonds	¼ tsp. onion powder
	2 tbsps. olive oil	¼ tsp. freshly ground black pepper
	1 tbsp. light brown sugar	⅛ tsp. garlic powder
	1 tsp. chopped fresh rosemary leaves	

1. In a large bowl, combine all the ingredients and toss until the nuts are evenly coated in the herbs, spices, and sugar.
2. Install a crisper plate in a basket. Scrape the nuts and seasonings into the basket, then insert basket in unit.
3. Select Zone 1, select AIR FRY, set temperature to 350°F, and set time to 6 minutes. Press the START/PAUSE button to begin cooking.
4. With 3 minutes remaining, press START/PAUSE to pause the unit. Remove the basket from unit and shake for 10 seconds. Reinsert basket in unit and press START/PAUSE to resume cooking, until golden brown and fragrant.
5. When cooking is complete, remove basket from unit. Transfer the cocktail nuts to a bowl and serve warm.

Buffalo Cauliflower with Sour Dip

PREP TIME: 10 minutes	1 large head cauliflower, separated into	⅔ cup nonfat Greek yogurt
COOK TIME: 20 minutes	small florets	½ tsp. Tabasco sauce
	1 tbsp. olive oil	1 celery stalk, chopped
	½ tsp. garlic powder	1 tbsp. crumbled blue cheese
	⅓ cup low-sodium hot wing sauce, divided	

1. Preheat the air fryer to 380ºF (193ºC).
2. In a large bowl, toss the cauliflower florets with the olive oil. Sprinkle with the garlic powder and toss again to coat.
3. Install a crisper plate in both baskets. Place half of the cauliflower in each basket.
4. Select Zone 1, select AIR FRY, set temperature to 390°F, and set time to 20 minutes. Select MATCH COOK to match Zone 2 settings to Zone 1. Select START/PAUSE to begin cooking.
5. When the Zone 1 and 2 times reach 10 minutes, press START/PAUSE to pause the unit. Remove the baskets from unit and shake for 10 seconds. Reinsert baskets in unit and press START/PAUSE to resume cooking.
6. When cooking is complete, transfer the cauliflower to a serving bowl and and toss with the wing sauce.
7. In a small bowl, stir together the yogurt, Tabasco sauce, celery, and blue cheese. Serve the cauliflower with the dip.

Chapter 11: Dessert

Cheesy Apple Roll-Ups

MAKES 8 ROLL-UPS

PREP TIME: 5 minutes
COOK TIME: 7 minutes

8 slices whole wheat sandwich bread
4 ounces (113 g) Colby Jack cheese, grated
½ small apple, chopped
2 tbsps. butter, melted

1. Remove the crusts from the bread and flatten the slices with a rolling pin. Don't be gentle. Press hard so that bread will be very thin.
2. Top bread slices with cheese and chopped apple, dividing the ingredients evenly.
3. Roll up each slice tightly and secure each with one or two toothpicks.
4. Brush outside of rolls with melted butter.
5. Install a crisper plate in both baskets. Place 4 rolls in a single layer in each basket.
6. Select Zone 1, select BAKE, set temperature to 390°F, and set time to 7 minutes. Select MATCH COOK to match Zone 2 settings to Zone 1. Select START/PAUSE to begin cooking.
7. When cooking is complete, transfer rolls to a plate. Serve warm.

Easy Chocolate Donuts

SERVES 8

PREP TIME: 5 minutes
COOK TIME: 10 minutes

1 (8-ounce / 227-g) can jumbo biscuits
Cooking oil
Chocolate sauce, for drizzling

1. Separate the biscuit dough into 8 biscuits and place them on a flat work surface. Use a small circle cookie cutter or a biscuit cutter to cut a hole in the center of each biscuit. You can also cut the holes using a knife.
2. Install a crisper plate in both baskets and spray with cooking oil. Place 4 donuts in a single layer in each basket.
3. Select Zone 1, select AIR FRY, set temperature to 375°F, and set time to 10 minutes. Select MATCH COOK to match Zone 2 settings to Zone 1. Select START/PAUSE to begin cooking.
4. When the Zone 1 and 2 times reach 5 minutes, press START/PAUSE to pause the unit. Remove the baskets from unit and flip the donuts over. Reinsert baskets in unit and press START/PAUSE to resume cooking.
5. When cooking is complete, transfer donuts to a plate. Drizzle chocolate sauce over the donuts and enjoy while warm.

Pecan Pie

PREP TIME: 10 minutes
COOK TIME: 35 minutes

⅓ cup butter, melted
2 large eggs
1¾ tbsps. flour
1 cup pecan halves
1 frozen pie crust, thawed
¾ cup brown sugar
¼ cup caster sugar
1 tsp. vanilla extract

1. Grease a 5-inch pie pan lightly.
2. Mix both sugars, eggs and butter in a bowl until smooth.
3. Stir in the flour, milk and vanilla extract and beat until well combined.
4. Fold in the pecan halves and arrange the crust in the bottom of pie pan. Put the pecan mixture in pie crust evenly.
5. Install a crisper plate in a basket. Place pie pan in the basket, then insert basket in unit.
6. Select Zone 1, select BAKE, set temperature to 300°F, and set time to 35 minutes. Press the START/PAUSE button to begin cooking.
7. With 15 minutes remaining, press START/PAUSE to pause the unit. Set the Air fryer to 285°F and press START/PAUSE to resume cooking.
8. When cooking is complete, remove basket from unit. Serve warm.

Homemade Apple Tart

PREP TIME: 15 minutes
COOK TIME: 25 minutes

2½-ounce butter, chopped and divided
3½-ounce flour
1 egg yolk
1 large apple, peeled, cored and cut into 12 wedges
1-ounce sugar

1. Grease a 7 x 5-inch baking pan lightly.
2. Mix half of the butter and flour in a bowl until a soft dough is formed.
3. Roll the dough into 6-inch round on a floured surface.
4. Place the remaining butter and sugar into the baking pan and arrange the apple wedges in a circular pattern.
5. Top with rolled dough and press gently along the edges of the pan.
6. Install a crisper plate in a basket. Place the baking pan in the basket, then insert basket in unit.
7. Select Zone 1, select BAKE, set temperature to 390°F, and set time to 25 minutes. Press the START/PAUSE button to begin cooking.
8. When cooking is complete, remove basket from unit. Serve warm.

Brownies Muffins

SERVES 12

PREP TIME: 10 minutes
COOK TIME: 13 minutes

1 package Betty Crocker fudge brownie mix
¼ cup walnuts, chopped
1 egg
2 tsps. water
⅓ cup vegetable oil

1. Grease 12 muffin molds lightly.
2. Mix all the ingredients in a bowl and divide evenly into the muffin molds.
3. Install a crisper plate in both baskets. Place half of the muffin molds in each basket.
4. Select Zone 1, select BAKE, set temperature to 300°F, and set time to 13 minutes. Select MATCH COOK to match Zone 2 settings to Zone 1. Select START/PAUSE to begin cooking.
5. When cooking is complete, dish out and invert the muffins onto wire rack to completely cool before serving.

Tasty Lemony Biscuits

SERVES 10

PREP TIME: 15 minutes
COOK TIME: 8 minutes

8½-ounce self-rising flour
3½-ounce cold butter
1 small egg
1 tsp. fresh lemon zest, grated finely
3½-ounce caster sugar
2 tbsps. fresh lemon juice
1 tsp. vanilla extract

1. Grease two 7 x 5-inch baking dishes lightly.
2. Mix flour and sugar in a large bowl.
3. Add cold butter and mix until a coarse crumb is formed.
4. Stir in the egg, lemon zest and lemon juice and mix until a dough is formed.
5. Press the dough into ½ inch thickness onto a floured surface and cut dough into medium-sized biscuits. Arrange the biscuits on the baking dishes in a single layer.
6. Install a crisper plate in both baskets. Place 1 baking dish in each basket.
7. Select Zone 1, select BAKE, set temperature to 355°F, and set time to 8 minutes. Select MATCH COOK to match Zone 2 settings to Zone 1. Select START/PAUSE to begin cooking, until golden brown.
8. When cooking is complete, transfer biscuits to a plate and serve with tea.

Bread Pudding

PREP TIME: 10 minutes
COOK TIME: 12 minutes

1 cup milk
1 egg
2 tbsps. raisins, soaked in hot water for about 15 minutes
2 bread slices, cut into small cubes
1 tbsp. chocolate chips
1 tbsp. brown sugar
½ tsp. ground cinnamon
¼ tsp. vanilla extract
1 tbsp. sugar

1. Grease a 7 x 5-inch baking dish lightly.
2. Mix milk, egg, brown sugar, cinnamon and vanilla extract until well combined.
3. Stir in the raisins and mix well.
4. Arrange the bread cubes evenly in the baking dish and top with the milk mixture.
5. Refrigerate for about 20 minutes and sprinkle with chocolate chips and sugar.
6. Install a crisper plate in a basket. Place the baking dish in the basket, then insert basket in unit.
7. Select Zone 1, select BAKE, set temperature to 375°F, and set time to 12 minutes. Press the START/PAUSE button to begin cooking.
8. When cooking is complete, remove basket from unit. Transfer bread pudding to a plate. Serve warm.

Peach Parcel

PREP TIME: 10 minutes
COOK TIME: 15 minutes

1 peach, peeled, cored and halved
1 cup prepared vanilla custard
2 puff pastry sheets
1 egg, beaten lightly
1 tbsp. sugar
Pinch of ground cinnamon
1 tbsp. whipped cream

1. Place a spoonful of vanilla custard and a peach half in the center of each pastry sheet.
2. Mix sugar and cinnamon in a bowl and sprinkle on the peach halves.
3. Pinch the corners of sheets together to shape into a parcel.
4. Install a crisper plate in a basket. Place parcels in the basket, then insert basket in unit.
5. Select Zone 1, select BAKE, set temperature to 340°F, and set time to 15 minutes. Press the START/PAUSE button to begin cooking.
6. When cooking is complete, remove basket from unit. Top with whipped cream.
7. Dish out and serve with remaining custard.

Simple Sweet Potato Soufflé

PREP TIME: 10 minutes
COOK TIME: 18 minutes

1 sweet potato, baked and mashed
2 tbsps. unsalted butter, divided
1 large egg, separated
¼ cup whole milk
½ tsp. kosher salt

1. In a medium bowl, combine the sweet potato, 1 tbsp. of melted butter, egg yolk, milk, and salt. Set aside.
2. In a separate medium bowl, whisk the egg white until stiff peaks form.
3. Using a spatula, gently fold the egg white into the sweet potato mixture.
4. Coat the inside of four 3-inch ramekins with the remaining 1 tbsp. of butter, then fill each ramekin halfway full.
5. Install a crisper plate in both baskets. Place 2 ramekins in a single layer in each basket.
6. Select Zone 1, select BAKE, set temperature to 330°F, and set time to 18 minutes. Select MATCH COOK to match Zone 2 settings to Zone 1. Select START/PAUSE to begin cooking.
7. When cooking is complete, remove the ramekins from the air fryer and allow to cool on a wire rack for 10 minutes before serving.

Stuffed Apples

PREP TIME: 10 minutes
COOK TIME: 13 minutes

4 small firm apples, cored
½ cup golden raisins
½ cup blanched almonds
4 tbsps. sugar, divided
½ cup whipped cream
½ tsp. vanilla extract

1. Grease a 7 x 5-inch baking dish lightly.
2. Put raisins, almond and half of sugar in a food processor and pulse until chopped.
3. Stuff the raisin mixture inside each apple and arrange the apples in the prepared baking dish.
4. Install a crisper plate in a basket. Place the baking dish in the basket, then insert basket in unit.
5. Select Zone 1, select BAKE, set temperature to 355°F, and set time to 10 minutes. Press the START/PAUSE button to begin cooking.
6. When cooking is complete, remove basket from unit.
7. Put cream, remaining sugar and vanilla extract on medium heat in a pan and cook for about 3 minutes, continuously stirring.
8. Remove from the heat and serve apple with vanilla sauce.

Appendix 1: 4-Week Meal Plan

Week-1	Breakfast	Lunch	Dinner	Snack/Dessert
Day-1	Tomato and Mozzarella Bruschetta	Leg of Lamb with Brussels Sprouts	Sweet and Sour Chicken Thighs	Cream Bread
Day-2	Ham, Spinach and Egg in a Cup	Cod and Veggies	Mustard Lamb Loin Chops	Coconut-Crusted Shrimp
Day-3	Golden Avocado Tempura	Broccoli with Olives	Pork Loin with Potatoes	Cheesy Steak Fries
Day-4	Tasty Toasts	Crispy Sirloin Steak	Crispy Cod Cakes with Salad Greens	Peach Parcel
Day-5	Ham and Corn Muffins	Chicken with Broccoli	Beef Cheeseburger Egg Rolls	Homemade Apple Tart
Day-6	Crispy Bread Rolls	Sweet and Sour Pork Chops	Perfectly Roasted Mushrooms	Bourbon Monkey Bread
Day-7	Jacket Potatoes	Fast Lamb Satay	Simple New York Strip Steak	Cheesy Hash Brown Bruschetta

Week-2	Breakfast	Lunch	Dinner	Snack/Dessert
Day-1	Yummy Breakfast Frittata	Herbed Turkey Breast	Beef and Vegetable Cubes	Eggnog Bread
Day-2	Tasty Toasts	Spicy Lamb Kebabs	Garden Fresh Veggie Medley	Cheesy Apple Roll-Ups
Day-3	Tomato and Mozzarella Bruschetta	Air Fried Crispy Chicken Tenders	Filling Pork Chops	English Pumpkin Egg Cake
Day-4	Sourdough Croutons	Italian Beef Meatballs	Amazing Salmon Fillets	Air Fried Pot Stickers
Day-5	Crispy Bread Rolls	Spices Stuffed Eggplants	Bacon Wrapped Pork Tenderloin	Simple Sweet Potato Soufflé
Day-6	Jacket Potatoes	Fantastic Leg of Lamb	Beef Chuck Cheeseburgers	Heavenly Tasty Lava Cake
Day-7	Ham, Spinach and Egg in a Cup	Herbed Haddock	Pesto Coated Rack of Lamb	Peppery Chicken Meatballs

Week-3	Breakfast	Lunch	Dinner	Snack/Dessert
Day-1	Lush Vegetable Omelet	Parmesan Asparagus	Spiced Lamb Steaks	Decadent Cheesecake
Day-2	Golden Avocado Tempura	Oats Crusted Chicken Breasts	Smoky Beef Burgers	Nutty Zucchini Bread
Day-3	Jacket Potatoes	Breaded Pork Chops and Parsnips	Okra with Green Beans	Lemony Pear Chips
Day-4	Yummy Breakfast Frittata	Italian Lamb Chops with Avocado Mayo	Cod with Asparagus	Easy Chocolate Donuts
Day-5	Ham, Spinach and Egg in a Cup	Crispy Chicken Drumsticks	Air Fried London Broil	Cream Bread
Day-6	Oat and Chia Porridge	Breaded Shrimp with Lemon	Pork Spare Ribs	Spiced Mixed Nuts
Day-7	Tasty Toasts	Tasty Beef Stuffed Bell Peppers	Sweet Chicken Kabobs	Heavenly Tasty Lava Cake

Week-4	Breakfast	Lunch	Dinner	Snack/Dessert
Day-1	Crispy Bread Rolls	Beef Tips with Onion	Sweet and Sour Brussels Sprouts	Sunflower Seeds Bread
Day-2	Ham and Corn Muffins	Beef Cheeseburgers	Air Fried Lamb Ribs	Buffalo Cauliflower with Sour Dip
Day-3	Yummy Breakfast Frittata	Super-Simple Scallops	Baked Chorizo Scotch Eggs	Air Fried Spicy Olives
Day-4	Lush Vegetable Omelet	Lamb with Potatoes	Buffalo Chicken Tenders	Bread Pudding
Day-5	Tomato and Mozzarella Bruschetta	Caramelized Carrots	Chicken and Veggie Kabobs	Rosemary Baked Cashews
Day-6	Sourdough Croutons	Potato and Prosciutto Salad	Garlic-Lemon Tilapia	Pecan Pie
Day-7	Golden Avocado Tempura	Spicy Chicken Legs	Buttered Filet Mignon	Simple Apple Cake

Appendix 2:
Basic Kitchen Conversions & Equivalents

DRY MEASUREMENTS CONVERSION CHART
3 teaspoons = 1 tablespoon = 1/16 cup
6 teaspoons = 2 tablespoons = 1/8 cup
12 teaspoons = 4 tablespoons = ¼ cup
24 teaspoons = 8 tablespoons = ½ cup
36 teaspoons = 12 tablespoons = ¾ cup
48 teaspoons = 16 tablespoons = 1 cup

METRIC TO US COOKING CONVERSIONS

OVEN TEMPERATURES
120 ºC = 250 ºF
160 ºC = 320 ºF
180 ºC = 350 ºF
205 ºC = 400 ºF
220 ºC = 425 ºF

LIQUID MEASUREMENTS CONVERSION CHART
8 fluid ounces = 1 cup = ½ pint = ¼ quart
16 fluid ounces = 2 cups = 1 pint = ½ quart
32 fluid ounces = 4 cups = 2 pints = 1 quart = ¼ gallon
128 fluid ounces = 16 cups = 8 pints = 4 quarts = 1 gallon

BAKING IN GRAMS
1 cup flour = 140 grams
1 cup sugar = 150 grams
1 cup powdered sugar = 160 grams
1 cup heavy cream = 235 grams

VOLUME
1 milliliter = 1/5 teaspoon
5 ml = 1 teaspoon
15 ml = 1 tablespoon
240 ml = 1 cup or 8 fluid ounces
1 liter = 34 fluid ounces

WEIGHT
1 gram = .035 ounces
100 grams = 3.5 ounces
500 grams = 1.1 pounds
1 kilogram = 35 ounces

US TO METRIC COOKING CONVERSIONS

1/5 tsp = 1 ml
1 tsp = 5 ml
1 tbsp = 15 ml
1 fluid ounces = 30 ml
1 cup = 237 ml
1 pint (2 cups) = 473 ml
1 quart (4 cups) = .95 liter
1 gallon (16 cups) = 3.8 liters
1 oz = 28 grams
1 pound = 454 grams

BUTTER
1 cup butter = 2 sticks = 8 ounces = 230 grams = 16 tablespoons

WHAT DOES 1 CUP EQUAL
1 cup = 8 fluid ounces
1 cup = 16 tablespoons
1 cup = 48 teaspoons
1 cup = ½ pint
1 cup = ¼ quart
1 cup = 1/16 gallon
1 cup = 240 ml

BAKING PAN CONVERSIONS
9-inch round cake pan = 12 cups
10-inch tube pan =16 cups
10-inch bundt pan = 12 cups
9-inch springform pan = 10 cups
9 x 5 inch loaf pan = 8 cups
9-inch square pan = 8 cups

BAKING PAN CONVERSIONS
1 cup all-purpose flour = 4.5 oz
1 cup rolled oats = 3 oz
1 large egg = 1.7 oz
1 cup butter = 8 oz
1 cup milk = 8 oz
1 cup heavy cream = 8.4 oz
1 cup granulated sugar = 7.1 oz
1 cup packed brown sugar = 7.75 oz
1 cup vegetable oil = 7.7 oz
1 cup unsifted powdered sugar = 4.4 oz

Appendix 3:
Ninja Dual Zone Air Fryer Timetable

Air Fry Cooking Chart

Ingredient	Amount Per Zone	Preparation	Temp	Single Zone	Dual Zone
VEGETABLES					
Asparagus	1 bunch	Whole, stems trimmed	390°F	8-12 mins	20-25 mins
Beets	6-7 small	Whole	390°F	30-35 mins	35-40 mins
Bell peppers (for roasting)	3 small peppers	Whole	390°F	10-15 mins	15-20 mins
Broccoli	1 head	Cut in 1-inch florets	390°F	8-10 mins	15-17 mins
Brussels sprouts	1 lb	Cut in half, stem removed	400°F	15-20 mins	20-25 mins
Butternut squash	1½ lbs	Cut in 1-2-inch pieces	390°F	20-25 mins	35-40 mins
Carrots	1 lb	Peeled, cut in ½-inch pieces	390°F	13-16 mins	25-30 mins
Cauliflower	1 head	Cut in 1-inch florets	390°F	17-20 mins	20-25 mins
Corn on the cob	2 ears, cut in half	Husks removed	390°F	12-15 mins	18-20 mins
Green beans	1 bag (12 oz)	Trimmed	390°F	8-10 mins	10-15 mins
Kale (for chips)	5 cups, packed	Torn in pieces, stems removed	300°F	7-9 mins	15-20 mins
Mushrooms	8 oz	Rinsed, cut in quarters	390°F	7-9 mins	13-15 mins
Potatoes, russet	1½ lbs	Cut in 1-inch wedges	400°F	20-22 mins	35-38 mins
	1 lb	Hand-cut fries, thin	400°F	20-24 mins	30-35 mins
	1 lb	Hand-cut fries, thick	400°F	19-24 mins	35-40 mins
	3 whole (6-8 oz)	Pierced with fork 3 times	400°F	30-35 mins	37-40 mins
Potatoes, sweet	1½ lbs	Cut in 1-inch chunks	400°F	15-20 mins	30-35 mins
	3 whole (6-8 oz)	Pierced with fork 3 times	400°F	36-42 mins	40-45 mins
Zucchini	1 lb	Cut in quarters lengthwise, then cut in 1-inch pieces	390°F	15-18 mins	25-28 mins
POULTRY					
Chicken breasts	2 breasts (¾-1½ lbs each)	Bone in	390°F	25-30 mins	30-35 mins
	4 breasts (½-¾ lb each)	Boneless	390°F	22-24 mins	25-28 mins
Chicken thighs	2 thighs (6-10 oz each)	Bone in	390°F	22-28 mins	26-29 mins
	4 thighs (4-8 oz each)	Boneless	390°F	18-22 mins	25-28 mins
Chicken wings	2 lbs	Drumettes & flats	390°F	18-22 mins	43-47 mins
FISH & SEAFOOD					
Crab cakes	2 cakes (6-8 oz each)	None	390°F	5-10 mins	10-13 mins
Lobster tails	4 tails (3-4 oz each)	Whole	390°F	5-8 mins	15-18 mins
Salmon fillets	3 fillets (4 oz each)	None	400°F	7-12 mins	13-17 mins
Shrimp	1 lb	Whole, peeled, tails	390°F	7-10 mins	10-13 mins
BEEF					
Burgers	2 quarter-pound patties, 80% lean	½ inch thick	390°F	8-10 mins	10-13 mins
Steaks	2 steaks (8 oz each)	Whole	390°F	10-20 mins	14-18 mins

PORK					
Bacon	3 strips, cut in half	None	350°F	8-10 mins	9-12 mins
Pork chops	2 thick-cut, bone-in chops (10-12 oz each)	Bone in	390°F	15-17 mins	23-27 mins
	2 boneless chops (8 oz each)	Boneless	390°F	14-17 mins	17-20 mins
Pork tenderloins	1 lb	None	375°F	15-20 mins	25-30 mins
Sausages	5 sausages	None	390°F	7-10 mins	17-22 mins
FROZEN FOODS					
Chicken cutlets	3 cutlets	None	400°F	18-21 mins	20-25 mins
Chicken nuggets	1 box (12 oz)	None	390°F	10-13 mins	18-21 mins
Fish fillets	1 box (6 fillets)	None	390°F	14-16 mins	17-22 mins
Fish sticks	18 fish sticks (11 oz)	None	390°F	10-13 mins	16-19 mins
French fries	1 lb	None	400°F	18-22 mins	28-32 mins
French fries	2 lbs	None	400°F	32-36 mins	50-55 mins
Mozzarella sticks	1 box (11 oz)	None	375°F	8-10 mins	10-12 mins
Pot stickers	2 bags (10.5 oz)	None	390°F	12-14 mins	16-18 mins
Pizza rolls	1 bag (20 oz, 40 count)	None	390°F	12-15 mins	15-18 mins
Popcorn shrimp	1 box (14-16 oz)	None	390°F	9-11 mins	14-18 mins
Sweet potato fries	1 lb	None	390°F	20-22 mins	30-32 mins
Tater tots	1 lb	None	375°F	18-22 mins	25-27 mins
Onion rings	10 oz	None	375°F	13-16 mins	18-22 mins

Dehydrate Chart

Ingredient	Preparation	Temp	Single Zone/Dual Zone
FRUITS & VEGETABLES			
Apples	Cored, cut in ⅛-inch slices, rinsed in lemon water, patted dry	135°F	7-8 hrs
Asparagus	Cut in 1-inch pieces, blanched	135°F	6-8 hrs
Bananas	Peeled, cut in ⅜-inch slices	135°F	8-10 hrs
Beets	Peeled, cut in ⅛-inch slices	135°F	6-8 hrs
Eggplant	Peeled, cut in ¼-inch slices, blanched	135°F	6-8 hrs
Fresh herbs	Rinsed, patted dry, stems removed	135°F	4 hrs
Ginger root	Cut in ⅜-inch slices	135°F	6 hrs
Mangoes	Peeled, cut in ⅜-inch slices, pit removed	135°F	6-8 hrs
Mushrooms	Cleaned with soft brush (do not wash)	135°F	6-8 hrs
Pineapple	Peeled, cored, cut in ⅜-½-inch slices	135°F	6-8 hrs
Strawberries	Cut in half or in ½-inch slices	135°F	6-8 hrs
Tomatoes	Cut in 3/8-inch slices or grated; steam if planning to rehydrate	135°F	6-8 hrs
MEAT, POULTRY, FISH			
Beef jerky	Cut in ¼-inch slices, marinated overnight	150°F	5-7 hrs
Chicken jerky	Cut in ¼-inch slices, marinated overnight	150°F	5-7 hrs
Turkey jerky	Cut in ¼-inch slices, marinated overnight	150°F	5-7 hrs
Salmon jerky	Cut in ¼-inch slices, marinated overnight	150°F	3-5 hrs

Appendix 4: Recipes Index

Made in the USA
Las Vegas, NV
09 December 2024

13689816R00044